MARIE DE FRANCE

Lais

Paula Clifford

Lecturer in French
University of Reading

Grant & Cutler Ltd
1982

I.S.B.N. 84-499-6032-0

DEPÓSITO LEGAL: V. 2.667 - 1982

Printed in Spain by
Artes Gráficas Soler, S.A., Valencia
for
GRANT & CUTLER LTD
11 BUCKINGHAM STREET, LONDON, W.C.2.

CONTENTS

Preface   7

1   Marie de France and the Breton Lay: the Prologue   9

2   The Force of Destiny: *Guigemar*   16

3   The Dilemma of Choice: *Chaitivel* and *Eliduc*   29

4   Obstacles to Love: *Equitan*, *Le Fresne*, *Milun*   44

5   Love and the Supernatural: *Lanval*, *Yonec*, *Bisclavret*   55

6   Aspects of Fatal Love: *Les deus amanz*, *Laüstic*, *Chevrefoil*   69

7   Marie's Contribution to Twelfth-Century Literature   78

    Bibliography   90

How is it under our control
To love or not to love?
Robert Browning

Preface

All textual references are to the edition of the *Lais* by A. Ewert (Oxford: Blackwell, 1963), last reprinted in 1978. The italicised figures in parentheses refer to numbered items in the Bibliography.

I have taught Marie de France's *Lais* for a number of years now, and I am grateful to my past students at the University of Reading for their stimulating reactions to the text, and to my former teachers at the University of Leeds who first aroused my interest in medieval French literature. I am particularly indebted to Professor Wolfgang van Emden who invited me to write this book and provided very many helpful suggestions and comments on the manuscript, although the responsibility for what it contains must ultimately be mine.

In the course of writing this book I produced a third child, and my unbounded thanks are due to my family and to many friends whose help and support enabled me to continue working. To them all this book is affectionately dedicated.

Paula Clifford
Reading, 1981.

1 *Marie de France and the Breton Lay: the Prologue*

(i) *Who was Marie de France?*

In the collection of *Lais* attributed to Marie de France we have one of those comparatively rare works of French literature whose influence on English writers has been considerable, and whose popularity on both sides of the Channel has been lasting. The genre which first enters literature with Marie's poems, although quite short-lived in France, inspired the admiration of Chaucer and his contemporaries, and led to a number of English imitations whose literary significance is indisputable. Yet, intriguingly, an air of mystery surrounds both the poetess and the provenance of her stories. We do not know who Marie was, or exactly when she composed her poems. Even after a hundred years of modern scholarship devoted to such questions, her identity and literary technique continue to excite critical comment and controversy.

Marie is still widely read, for the simple reasons that her subject, love, is eternally popular, and that in illustrating love's aspects she has some good tales to tell. The language of the original, the twelfth-century Anglo-Norman dialect of medieval French, is not particularly difficult to read, not least because Marie normally eschews the complex turn of phrase and elaborate vocabulary. Some of her poems, such as *Laüstic*, the story of the nightingale, or the episode in the saga of Tristan and Isolde, *Chevrefoil*, have attracted greater attention than others, by virtue of their more general thematic appeal, and as a result surveys of the text have not always given each poem equal consideration. The aim of the present study is to focus on the collection of *Lais* in the Harley manuscript (the source of Ewert's edition) as a whole, and to discuss the unity of inspiration and style that underlies the individual poems. In the light of this I shall hope to show how Marie's contribution to twelfth-century literature is unique, both with respect to her own methods of composition and to her original treatment of common themes and motifs.

Who, then, was Marie de France? It seems to be widely, although not universally, accepted that she was a real person, and that she wrote not just the *Lais*, but also, subsequently, the *Fables* (a translation of Aesopic and other tales) and a moralizing poem, the *Espurgatoire S. Patrice*, based on a Latin *Tractatus*. Ewert (p. viii) explains that this last work must have been written after 1189, since it contains a reference to a saint who was canonized in that year. This is little enough, but there is even less evidence for a precise dating of the earlier works. The *Lais* are dedicated to an unnamed king, and again it is widely accepted that this was Henry II of England, and that Marie was in some way connected with his court. The court of Henry and Eleanor of Aquitaine, who married in 1152, was an itinerant one, fostering literary and artistic talent up to the time of the Queen's imprisonment in 1173, and it seems reasonable to suppose that the *Lais* were composed at some time between these dates, although they could have been written as late as 1189, the year of Henry's death. Further, it is also supposed that Marie knew of, and was influenced by, the *Brut* of Wace, which appeared in 1155, an imaginative history ranging from the fall of Troy to the creation of Saxon England, and significant for its inclusion of the legend of King Arthur and his Round Table (see further Pelan, *41*). It is thought too that Chrétien de Troyes may have been familiar with the *Lais* when he wrote his *Erec et Enide* in 1170. The results of research in the last fifteen years or so have tended to place the composition date of the *Lais* slightly earlier than did previous scholars, Ringger, for example (*43*, p. 13), suggesting a time between 1155 and 1165. In all probability, as Illingworth has convincingly demonstrated (*35*), the poems were written in two groups, one of which draws more extensively on literary allusion than the other, and was probably written later, and these were then set in order by Marie, who added the final touch to her collection, a prologue. This hypothesis has, however, been forcefully rejected by Baum (*3*, p. 218), who insists, rather perversely, that there is no evidence for regarding the collection as the work of a single author, or that this author was called Marie, although Ringger (*43*, p. 103) disagrees for structural and thematic reasons similar to my own. However, various identities have been proposed for Marie, and it must be said that none of them is particularly convincing. The poems themselves lend strong support to the notion that she was familiar with aristocratic life and behaviour, and that she was writing for a so-called courtly, perhaps largely female, audience. In common with her illustrious contemporaries, Chrétien de Troyes, Béroul and Thomas, her success lies in the way in which she transforms the material of folklore and legend so as to satisfy the new and changing preoccupations of a literary public in the second half of the twelfth century.

(ii) *The Breton Lay*

The question 'Who was Marie de France?' is unlikely to be answered without some new evidence from her own time. On the other hand, the question 'What was a Breton lay?' is perhaps easier to answer. Certainly it is not hard to gather what Marie understood by the original term *lai*, for she refers to the characteristics of their composition in most of her poems. The essential elements are reiterated by Chaucer in his prologue to *The Franklin's Tale*:

> Of old the noble Bretons in their days
> Delighted in adventures and made lays
> In rhyme, according to their early tongue,
> Which to the sound of instruments were sung... (*11*)

Thus the lay is traditionally an adventure of ancient origin recounted in verse and set to music. With Marie de France, however, the lay has undergone a distinct change in direction. The lays she claims for her sources were above all musical compositions which, like the modern popular song, could be performed as a purely instrumental melody on the harp or *rote*. C. Bullock-Davies (*8*, p. 21) has also suggested that this music had specific formal features of its own, differentiating it from other styles of composition. Marie's contribution is to emphasize the adventure, thereby creating a narrative poem which was to be recited or read rather than sung. This additional meaning of the term 'lay' was obviously familiar to Chaucer, and may even have been the dominant quality, for his prologue cited above continues, somewhat anachronistically:

...Or read in silence for their own delight.

Clearly in the absence of more detailed information about the oral tradition of the time, we cannot be certain that Marie alone was responsible for this new literary form, but her work seems to be the first evidence we have of it.

The etymology of the word *lai*, which in Marie's poems becomes synonymous with *conte*, is not wholly clear, but a number of critics draw attention to the Old Irish *laíd* or *loíd*, which, according to Rachel Bromwich (*6*, p. 36), were prose interludes inserted in Old Irish verse sagas. It is perhaps significant that the only form of Celtic literature con-temporaneous with Marie should have this cognate term in its vocabulary, for what is certain is that no specifically Breton lays survive, and that by Breton, Marie in fact means Celtic. Tales of Celtic origin may have come to her through that part of Celtic tradition with which she would have been familiar, the legends of Armorican Brittany. It seems likely that Marie heard only the stories and not the music, although she would have been aware of its existence, and that for her *li Breton* are synonymous with *li ancien*. Her purpose in the *Lais* is to recast stories with a common theme, some of which may indeed have belonged to a lost literature, while for others she claims similar antiquity and authority. We shall see later how Marie seeks to authenticate her tales by including, where possible, topographical details of Britanny and Breton names or other linguistic forms. The Breton connection is, however, at times rather forced, the setting being often irrelevant or not even Breton at all: the *lai* of *Les deus amanz* takes place in Normandy. The *Lais* of the Harley manuscript are given the title *Lais de Bretagne*, but it is impossible to say whether the poetess herself or a scribe is responsible for this.

Marie's use of the term *lai* is ambiguous. On the one hand it refers to her source, and on the other it is used specifically of her own work, the *conte* which she has made out of the original *lai*.

But Marie's poems are not just shorter versions of the new *roman courtois*, for they retain some quite specific features of the older form. The characteristic content of Marie's *lais* may be summed up as a love-related adventure of long ago, often containing elements from Breton, or more generally Celtic tradition, particularly magical or supernatural motifs. The term 'adventure' also requires some explanation. Clearly some of the longer *lais* are adventures in the conventional sense: one thinks of the trials of the characters in *Guigemar*, *Yonec* or *Milun*. Elsewhere, however, much less occurs; the stories of *Laüstic*, *Chevrefoil* and *Chaitivel* are single happenings: the killing of a bird, the isolated meeting of a pair of lovers, the death of knights in a tournament — none of them world-shaking events. Here again Marie has taken an accepted literary term and turned it to her own use, for in each poem the central issue is an 'adventure', major or minor, in the characters' experience of love.

Marie's art in the *Lais* (unlike the *Fables*) is to bring to this base what is at first sight a hotchpotch of other literary elements. Borrowings from Classical authors, notably Ovid (see pp.24-25 below), and Biblical allusions are combined with local legend, fairy stories, Arthurian tradition and thematic and linguistic borrowing from her immediate forerunners in French literature, the *romans d'antiquité* of the 1150s. If all this seems not to merit a claim of originality for Marie, it must be remembered that the art of twelfth-century literature lies in the creative retelling of what is often already well-known, as Spearing (*46*, p. 22) has pointed out: 'In the works of the best medieval poets the conventional ways of expression are modified and extended as well as being repeated'. Thus Marie's audience appreciated the interplay of familiar symbols and allusions from disparate sources, in a way in which the twentieth-century reader, brought up to believe that new is beautiful, may find hard to understand.

Such was the influence of Marie that, as we have seen, the term *lai* is used subsequently to refer primarily to a narrative tale. It seems likely that her poems immediately inspired imitations, and we have the texts of a number of *Lais anonymes* dating from the late twelfth and early thirteenth centuries.

Several of these have been attributed to Marie herself at some time or another, but critical opinion has tended towards the view that their authors are generally less skilful than Marie as far as style and technique are concerned, although certain similarities may be perceived. The editor of a recent collection of such poems has drawn attention to a basic thematic difference: Marie's first imitators were mainly interested in an atmosphere of mystery created by the use of supernatural motifs, whereas in Marie's work, where such motifs occur, they are always subsidiary to the psychological analysis of action and characters (*49*, pp. 79 and 81). All in all, Marie is adjudged superior in style and characterization as well as in her use of literary tradition. As far as the *lais* composed at a later date are concerned, the thematic link with Marie seems to be reduced to that of a background of courtliness, against which any adventure may take place.

(iii) *The Prologue to Marie's 'Lais'*

The Prologue which introduces the twelve *lais* has several important functions, not the least of which is to confer unity on the collection of poems as a whole. The fact that it exists only in the Harley manuscript, and also that Marie appears to have adopted the common authorial practice of writing her introduction after completing the rest of the work, should not be reasons for doubting its authenticity. Indeed, despite some uncharacteristic obscurities in expression, it is a good example both of Marie's style and of her technique as a story-teller, in that here, as in the *Lais* themselves, she can be seen to be borrowing from other writers and traditions, and intermingling her sources to suit her own ends.

The first forty-two lines of the Prologue are concerned broadly with Marie's justification of her work, while the remaining fourteen lines form the dedication already mentioned. This leads on at once to the first *lai* in the collection, *Guigemar*, which has a twenty-six line prologue of its own before the story begins. Although some critics including Delbouille (*18*) have seen in this a prologue to the entire collection, since it occurs first in all but the Harley manuscript, it must, I think, be regarded as a further unifying factor in Marie's composition. In it, the author moves from the generalities of the first Prologue to a more particular statement of her intentions, identifying herself ('ke dit Marie'), her audience ('oëz seigneurs') and her subject matter ('les contes...dunt li Bretun unt fait les lais'), which leads quite naturally into the first story. Again, the likely hypothesis advanced by some scholars, that *Guigemar* was written after some of the other *lais*, should not trouble us unduly. The critic's primary task must be the appreciation of the text before him, and *Guigemar* is, in any case, a very suitable poem with which to begin.

The first part of the Prologue (9-27) is roughly translated in Ewert's edition, and raises several interpretative problems. These are discussed fully and clearly in an article by Tony Hunt (*33*), which the reader is recommended to consult. From line 47 it is obvious that Marie envisaged a collection of poems, whether or not it is the one before us now, and this is borne out elsewhere in the openings to *Bisclavret*, *Yonec*, *Milun* and *Lanval*. Her double task of telling and rhyming the stories is important to her (cf. 39-41, 48), and the overall effect is perhaps to convey something of the author's enthusiasm for her task and excitement at her opportunity to carry it out. She addresses the King respectfully in her dedication, using terms which are elsewhere applied to her fictional heroes and heroines, *nobles*, *pruz*, *curteis*, and indicating his special nature as the fount of goodness (45-46), so that the graceful homage of lines 52-55 does not come amiss. While, therefore, the Prologue fulfils a necessary literary function, Marie's personality and poetic technique already lend it the stamp of her individuality. Although literary allusions are more abundant here, in a short space, than elsewhere, they do not conceal Marie's purpose. In the last fourteen lines we glimpse the deceptively simple use of clear language that is her hallmark in the *lais* that follow.

2 *The Force of Destiny:* Guigemar

(i) *The conventions of courtly love in contemporary writing*

The literature of what modern scholars have termed 'courtly' love is not confined to a single period or country. It is a European phenomenon which spanned three centuries, and whose precise origins are unclear. Courtly love poetry appears for the first time in Provençal literature in the last decades of the eleventh century with no apparent precursors either in Provence or elsewhere, although a strong argument may be made for the influence of Arab-dominated Spain in the previous century (cf. Briffault, *5*). In Provence, courtly love found its expression almost uniquely in the lyric poetry of the troubadours, the finest of whom were writing in the last thirty years or so of the twelfth century, before the Albigensian crusade put an abrupt end to their activities a few years later. By this time, however, the new movement had spread into Northern France, as well as into Spain, Catalonia and Northern Italy, and from France into Germany and Britain. A short survey of the doctrine of courtly love may be found in Denomy (*19*).

Although Provençal poetry was to serve as the model for courtly writing elsewhere, it was by no means slavishly imitated, a notable exception to this being the work of some Catalan and Italian poets, who went so far as to adopt the Provençal language for their purpose. In Northern France ideas of courtly love were assimilated into a more strongly narrative literary tradition and were consequently developed much more fully than had been possible within the narrow limits of a lyric poem. Certainly in the course of the twelfth century the Provençal poets came to adhere to a very rigid set of literary conventions in their treatment of love, and the greatest of them can only be defined according to the degree of artistic and stylistic variation they achieved within these limits. It seems probable that the genre would have degenerated into complete sterility, had not social and political forces put an abrupt end to the courts which had fostered it. In the same way, then, that the originality of a troubadour may be judged by the degree of individuality he displays in writing according to clearly defined rules, so the originality of a poet such as Marie de France may be gauged to some extent by the use she makes of the new literary form presented to her. We shall see that while Marie's heroes and heroines are in a sense 'courtly', the freedom of action granted them sets them in a world apart from their Provençal prototypes, a world altogether more realistic, sensitive and humane.

The classic courtly relationship depicted in the Provençal *canso* (love song), which is the most common poetic form used by the troubadours and the one they most cultivated and admired, depends on three things: the supremacy and aloofness of the *dompna* (lady), the total subservience of her would-be lover, and the ennobling power of *fin'amors* (ideal love), which the lover strives to achieve. The poet receives no reward for his pains, except the *joia* which comes from the perfect service of his lady, who, it is assumed, will eventually be obliged to bestow her favours on him. Even a cursory examination of the characters of the lovers and the nature of their love in Marie's poems will show how far she has deviated from the troubadour ideal, or adapted it to suit her own ends.

The Provençal *dompna* is the creation of a literature written primarily for and about the aristocracy. Here there is, of course, a similarity with Marie's work, for she sets her characters in the context she knows best, that of the court, and most of them are noble by birth or hold an exalted social position. But this is as far as the parallel goes, for the feelings and actions of Marie's couples are such that they may be universally understood and appreciated. It is usually assumed that the troubadour's lady was married (although relatively few poems actually refer to a husband), and that the poet creates a fantasy based on his idealization of an adulterous relationship. Thus, because of her marriage and of her social status, which is necessarily superior to that of the poet, the troubadour is bound by secrecy. He must not reveal his lady's real name and must observe discretion at all times. This last quality (*mezura*) is an important one, and in Marie de France it becomes an essential ingredient in all successful relationships, whether between lovers (e.g. *Lanval*, *Yonec*) or not (e.g. the father-daughter relationship in *Les deus amanz*). The troubadour's lady is a mysterious creature; since the poems are concerned mainly with the emotions of the poet himself, we know nothing of her feelings. When the poet is unsuccessful he will describe her as proud and cruel, so that it appears almost to be in her nature to be so, an attitude condemned by Marie in *Chaitivel*. Her physical appearance is described in fairly stereotyped terms (cf. Cropp, *15*), and that she is beautiful goes without saying. Marie, too, is not over-concerned with the appearance of her women, although for her, beauty and courtliness by no means go together (e.g. the lady in *Bisclavret*). The 'portrait' is not fully developed until, as Colby (*12*) has demonstrated, Chrétien de Troyes makes it an integral part of the style of his courtly romances.

In giving us closer insight into the feelings of her ladies, Marie is more realistic in her treatment both of women and of the love relationship. The only remote parallel in Provençal lies in the poems of the female troubadours, the *trobairitz*, who probably wrote after Marie, and who give an account of their own feelings in the face of unrequited or unsuccessful love, which is not quite the same as a true insight into the sentiments of the troubadour's *dompna*. As we shall see, Marie's women are capable of displaying a wide range of emotions and are quite unpredictable in their behaviour—a force to be reckoned with.

In view of this more realistic and humanized approach to love, it is not surprising to find that Marie is interested in a relationship between equals, and that her men do not grovel for favours: if they do, disaster ensues (cf. *Chaitivel* and *Equitan*). For the most part (with the exception of *Equitan*, and, initially, apparently, *Le Fresne*) we are dealing with love between social equals. It is just as important that the man should be *curteis* as it is for the lady. The idea that through his love a man may better himself is therefore discarded, and realism demands that he should not find complete fulfilment simply in desiring his lady in

the requisite manner. Marie's lovers enter quite unambiguo
into a physical relationship with no concern for the Churc
teaching either on marriage or adultery. Even where it might oe
possible, marriage is not the supreme end for her couples, which
is no doubt realistic, but also more daring than in a writer such
as Chrétien, who is altogether more discreet. On the other hand,
Marie's characters do not indulge in sex indiscriminately. Their
relationship is carefully prepared, with great emphasis laid on
the suitability of the couple, and their mutual love and esteem.
When Marie considers her couples in some way incompatible or
immoral, in her own terms, they are punished (see further
pp.78-82)

The final modification made to the courtly love conventions
by Marie and by her contemporary writers of romance in
Northern France is the integration of the well-established ideals
of chivalry. Action in Provençal courtly poetry is virtually non-
existent, although, later, the notion of the *asag*, a test or trial for
the lover, does arrive from the North. In Marie de France's work
love and action are inseparable, which enables her to explore
fully many facets of human love in very different contexts.

(ii) *Guigemar*

It is fitting that *Guigemar* should head the collection of *lais*, for
in the course of this fairly uncomplicated love story, we are
shown very clearly crucial differences between Marie's
characters and the stereotypes of the Provençal courtly lyric.
Obviously the groups into which I have divided the twelve *lais*
are not self-contained units. Many elements studied in later
chapters are therefore to be found also in *Guigemar*, particularly
the supernatural and certain obstacles to love, but the dominant
theme strikes me as that of destiny. Marie is thus able to study in
detail the nature of love itself, and once her more flexible
treatment of the love relationship has been established through
this opening *lai*, she is able to examine many variations in
situation and character in those that follow.

In *Guigemar* Marie presents a pair of worthy and ultimately
courtly lovers, who act out a thoroughly realistic drama, which

significantly, has its roots in a mutual physical attraction. In contrast to the single viewpoint of troubadour poetry, the *lai* of *Guigemar* is concerned as much with the unnamed mistress as with the hero himself. The lady is carefully shown not to be proud, but rather she is warmhearted and displays considerable emotion when confronted with the apparently dead body of an unknown knight. Furthermore, she is far from being passive, but, unperturbed by the perils of a magic voyage, is quite capable of looking after herself. As for Guigemar, he is not, unlike the lady, described initially as *curteis*, in view of his inability to love, a necessary prerequisite for courtliness in Marie's eyes. The story describes the process by which he achieves courtliness, first in loving his lady and then in his prowess on her behalf. The couple are thus of equal standing both in their love for each other and in their subsequent actions. Since Marie is not interested in unfulfilled longing, her concept of *joie* resides in the lovers' happy, though secret, physical union. Even the jealous husband is given a slightly more active role than troubadour poetry could allow him. It is he who causes the lovers to part, but not before listening to Guigemar's story and granting him the chance to leave if he can find his magic boat. Similarly, Meriadus, the lady's captor and would-be lover, does not give her up without a fight. Thus concern for characterization and the element of adventure both add depth to the lovers' story, which is accorded a sympathetic and original treatment.

While the title of the *lai* indicates that the poem recounts Guigemar's story, I would not, as I have already hinted, go as far as Sienaert (*45*, p. 51), who maintains that the hero is the only important character in it. His name is Breton in form, supporting Marie's claim that the action took place 'en Bretaigne la menur' (25). However, its similarity to the form 'Guingamor' presents us with the possibility of two separate underlying adventures. In the anonymous *lai* of *Guingamor* (see *47*), the hero receives the love of a fairy, and in Chrétien's *Erec* there is also a reference to a knight named Guigomar, Lord of Avalon and 'friend' of Morgan le Fay. Although I would not wish to maintain that Guigemar's lady is other worldly, there are parallels between the two stories, mainly in the motifs of the hunt and the magic voyage. The second part of Marie's *lai*, however, which concerns the lovers' adventures and eventual reunion, has little which is typically Celtic. Making this point, Illingworth (*34*, p. 187) concludes that 'a composite Breton story was further modified by Marie herself under the influence of Old French literary fashions', and we shall see further evidence of this influence in due course. The prologue to the *lai* has already been mentioned in the last chapter, although it is worth noting again Marie's self-confidence in the face of the possible jealousy of 'gangleür u losengier' (16), mockers or slanderers, who, in Provençal literature, are conventionally opposed to any expression of courtly love.

All Marie's *lais* show a concern for coherent structured narration, and *Guigemar* falls neatly into three sections of approximately equal length. Part I, containing allegorical and supernatural themes, tells of Guigemar's wound and magic voyage before he meets his lady, part II forms the central love episode, while part III recounts the lovers' adventures after their separation, and their eventual reunion. At the beginning of the story (27-68) Marie introduces her hero as a knight of the highest order and there is an unusual amount of detail concerning his family background. Line 27 specifies the setting of the *lai* in Arthurian times, and lines 29-32 reveal a close association between Guigemar's father and a prestigious ruler, who is close to Arthur himself. Hoilas, referred to in Geoffrey of Monmouth's *History* as Hoel the Great (*28*, p. 254), was Arthur's nephew. Thus Marie is not only evoking an Arthurian background through this reference, but, by indicating a certain intimacy between Hoilas and Oridials, is indirectly asking us to consider Guigemar as worthy as any of the more famous knights of the Round Table.

Although Guigemar's family is a happy one, to which he is glad to return (69-75), there is nothing to suggest, *pace* Green (*29*, p. 325), undue dominance on the part of his mother and sister. However, although the young knight is attractive to women, he shows no sign of wanting their love, with the result that he is thought to be *peri* (67). Critics (e.g. Pickens, *42*) have suggested that this is a euphemism for homosexuality, and have interpreted much of the *lai* as an account of the hero's sexual problems. Yet while it is quite possible that Guigemar could have been slandered in this way (and we see the theme of slander also spelt out in *Le Fresne* and *Les deus amanz*, whereas in troubadour writing the concept is usually left vague), I cannot accept that the adventure arises primarily out of Guigemar's sexual inadequacy and social ineffectiveness. This comment seems to me typical of Marie's concern for realistic detail, and Guigemar's apparent shortcomings are soon to be resolved in a very special love affair, for which, perhaps, nature has reserved him. When this happens, Guigemar, like the anonymous knight in Jehan Renart's *Lai de l'ombre*, falls all the harder because of his previous resistance to love.

The first stage in the main action of the *lai* (69-122) is a hunt. This is, of course, a standard device in romance tradition for introducing adventures which very often have supernatural features, and its importance is reflected in the amount of detail which Marie accords it. Then there is the equally familiar figure of the white stag, whose function is generally to introduce the hero to another world (cf. Webster, *50*). As Paton (*39*, p. 67) has pointed out, the hind ought to have been a transformed fairy, but there seems little justification for this here. The arrow with which Guigemar wounds the hind is, of course, also symbolic of the arrow of love, and love now takes revenge on the hero as it rebounds and wounds him in the thigh. This is a favourite mishap in romance, for it incapacitates without being fatal, and may also carry sexual connotations. Guigemar falls from his horse alongside the hind, who is described as *nafree* (103) and *anguissuse* (104), a significant use of vocabulary, since it is precisely these terms which will be used later to describe Guigemar's emotional anguish (381, 394). The language of suffering is always ambiguous in courtly literature (see further Burgess, *9*), and this is a neat example of its exploitation.

The speech of the wounded hind is the first overt expression of the supernatural in this *lai*, yet it is presented without comment, and the animal's judgement is accepted unquestioningly and with dismay, rather than surprise, on the part of Guigemar. This tacit acceptance of magical elements by Marie (and her hero) is a typical feature of her style; as an essentially realistic writer she refrains from drawing attention to details which are necessary to her story but defy rational explanation. Above all, the supernatural part of this *lai* has the function of ensuring that the hero meets his lady, and so he sets off through a landscape whose appearance is typically that of a passage from this world to another (cf. *Lanval*, 44-45, and *Yonec*, 336). Yet these features have a practical purpose as well: the wood effectively separates Guigemar from his fellow huntsmen and the water leads him to the harbour with its magic boat. In Marie's poems, therefore, the supernatural is never gratuitous, and is included only insofar as it is directly related to the exposition of the main situation. Once Guigemar arrives at his lady's home, the only task remaining to otherworldly forces is to provide boats for the lovers' separate escapes.

The description of the magic boat has been the subject of much critical comment. The overall effect is one of supreme richness (158) and this is a characteristic of the supernatural also in the description of the fairy's abode in *Lanval* (80-92). The boat has several apparently magical features: it is made without obvious join (155-56) and has fittings of ebony, an exotic wood which, as Mickel (*37*) has shown, may also have mystical associations. The description of the bed inside it is reminiscent both of a description in the *Eneas* (cf. Hoepffner *31*, pp. 279-82) and of a passage in the *Song of Songs*, evoked by the name of Solomon, in which the King has a magnificent litter to carry him to the bridal bed (3. 7-10). Marie, then, follows the twelfth-century fashion for describing rich and exotic objects, comparing her things of great beauty and miraculous events to universally accepted marvels, not always to the credit of the latter. In this boat Guigemar is carried out to sea, being too absorbed in his surroundings and his pain to notice the movement. When he arrives at the capital of an unnamed kingdom, Marie tells us that he will be cured there, and the function of the supernatural is virtually over.

At line 209 the direction of the narrative changes with the introduction of a *mal-mariée*, a familiar character type in

medieval literature, although there is little evidence of
stereotyping in Marie's description of her. It is significant that
we are first presented with a married couple whose union is
considered unsuitable, before the courtship of another pair is
described, who are well-matched, even though the lady is
married. The husband is old and, therefore, 'gelus esteit a
desmesure' (213), two typically uncourtly features. Against this
is set the courtliness of his wife: she is well-bred and 'franche,
curteise, bele e sage' (212), a combination of epithets which is
enough to indicate Marie's approval. She is comparable to
Fresne, who is 'bele e enseignee/sage, curteise e afeitee' (*Le
Fresne*, 253-54), but unlike the lady in *Chaitivel*, who only
partially fulfils the conditions: 'Une dame que mut valeit/De
beauté e d'enseignement/E de tut bon affeitement' (*Chaitivel*,
10-12). The lady in *Guigemar* is kept closely guarded, her only
freedom being in a closed garden, the sea being considered,
ironically, a safe barrier on one side (225). It is worth noting that
where a parallel situation exists in *Yonec*, it is resolved by the
arrival of a supernatural being, while in *Guigemar* the magic lies
in the bringing together of two ordinary mortals. The only
access to the lady's bedroom is through a chapel (232), possibly
a hint of a test to evil spirits, similar to that in *Yonec*, where the
magic knight volunteers to receive Holy Communion as a proof
of his goodness.

Line 239 has a reference to 'Le livre Ovide' which is of two-
fold significance. Firstly, in the context of the *lai*, the lady's
bedroom is seen to be decorated with pictures of Venus
instructing lovers and rejecting Ovid's *Remedia Amoris*, which
tells how love may be overcome. This detail is perhaps
ambiguous: is the husband encouraging his wife's feelings
towards himself, or is it suggesting that she will be receptive to
the love of another? Secondly, the allusion to Ovid makes
explicit the notion of Ovidian love which is manifest in some of
the *lais* through the themes and imagery which Marie uses.
Robathan (*44*, pp. 199-200) has drawn attention to the
importance of the *Eneas* (*20*) in this respect, which combined
material from Virgil and Ovid, and which undoubtedly
influenced contemporary writers. In Marie's work, images such

as the idea of love as a sickness or as a wounding arrow are drawn from the Classical poet either directly or via other sources. Other minor characters are then introduced. The first is a worthy maiden, the lady's companion; they are related by marriage and enjoy a close friendship, which will facilitate the lady's infidelity. The second is a guard figure, a eunuch priest, described rather graphically by Marie (255-60). His function is to cater for the lady's spiritual and material needs, and he is clearly not seen as a serious threat.

With Marie's exposition complete we are prepared for the long central love episode (261-534), which is remarkable for its sympathetic description of the gradual awakening of feelings of love in both characters, and which has a close parallel in *Eliduc*. This is a good illustration of the way in which Marie draws on Ovidian ideas in putting her sentimental theory into practice. Guigemar, who recognizes what is happening to him, fears above all the lady's possible pride, and the danger of pride is of course highlighted in the hero's peculiar situation, in that his life depends on the nature of the woman he is beginning to love. He also accepts the necessity of suffering in love, thereby acknowledging further helplessness. Yet this is not the subservience of a troubadour: it is the understandable reaction of a man in love for the first time, whose feelings are emphasized by the complexity of the situation in which he finds himself. After a sleepless night his torment is reflected in his facial appearance, and we know at once that the lady's sufferings are similar, because her *semblant* too is changed and remarked on. The maidservant's role is to be both Guigemar's more experienced *confidante* and also Marie de France's mouthpiece. She tells Guigemar to beware of reticence (446) because he and her mistress make an ideal couple. This is summed up in her line 'Vus estes bels e ele est bele' (453), which, I think, should not be taken as meaning just physical appearance but a mutual compatibility in all aspects of their characters. The fact that the girl is correct in her assessment is stressed by the reiteration of her own qualities: 'Mut ert curteise e deboneire' (464).

Guigemar's declaration of love and his eventual acceptance is introduced by the detail that the lady first heard Mass. Although

Marie is advocating a view of love alien to the teaching of the Church, she is often at pains to point out that she sees no conflict between religious beliefs and her couples' conduct. When eventually Guigemar plucks up courage to tell the lady of his physical and emotional dependance on her, his 'jeo meorc pur vus' (501) has both literal and figurative significance. The lady's reply 'en riant' delays the outcome only a little, but gives Guigemar the opportunity to put forward some newfound insights into the nature of women. He claims that only a fickle woman keeps a man on tenterhooks and concludes, again ambiguously, 'finum cest plait!' (526). The lady concurs, and Marie ends with a short celebration of physical love. Thus at this point Guigemar has matured into a successful lover, and the abstract notions of courtly love have been worked out in concrete form.

At the beginning of the final part of the *lai* (535-883) several details indicate a complete break with the story so far. Firstly there is a time lapse (535, 545) and secondly there is a brief change to allegorical language in the reference to the wheel of fortune (538-40), as Marie anticipates the lovers' separation. The theme of death, previously expressed only by Guigemar, is now taken up by his mistress, but this time in terms of their mutual fate, which is reminiscent of the recurring theme in Tristan literature (cf. *Chevrefoil*, 67). It is to allay the lady's fear of losing Guigemar to another woman that the lovers go through a form of exchange of tokens. The knot in the shirt and the lady's belt will serve as recognition devices to the lovers and also as a form of test to others. Both are clearly intended as chastity belts, which assist the lovers' loyalty to each other. The discovery scene is important in that for the first time since Guigemar was wounded we are reminded of his valour as a knight and of his prowess which seems undiminished. When Guigemar returns home he is greeted as a long lost hero and now, still attractive to women, he has good reason for rejecting them. From all over the country they come to try to undo the knot in his shirt, a reversal of more common tradition where it is the knights who test their skill with a lady.

Guigemar's departure is described in approximately thirty

lines, and it is indicative of the importance attached to the role of the lady in this *lai* that her adventures occupy the next hundred lines and that she continues to dominate the scene in the final episode dealing with the lovers' reunion. The narrative moves swiftly towards its dénouement, aided by the return of a hint of the supernatural which, as in *Yonec* (336-40) allows the lady to escape. Her virtual capture by Meriadus enables Marie to present us with an uncourtly rival to Guigemar. Meriadus, who attempts to undo the lady's belt by force, seems to be attracted only by her beauty and his obsession with her is such that he refuses to give her up (704, 708). The tournament which precipitates the recognition scene serves as a further reminder of Guigemar's valour, for Meriadus is anxious to have him on his side. Despite the existence of recognition devices it is significant, and perhaps more realistic, that Guigemar should recognize his mistress by her *semblant* and *manere* (771), although it is also quite likely that after some time (743) Guigemar would not entirely trust his first impressions. His self-questionings continue to be couched in the courtly language that characterized the earlier relationships (773-75), and while the remark that 'femmes se resemblent asez' (779) may seem uncourtly, it echoes a familiar motif in medieval romance that women are not always who they appear to be (cf. the false Guinevere in Arthurian literature and the deceptions of Morgan le Fay).

The final episode, where the lady has to undergo the test of the knot, is dominated by conflicting emotions: the alternating doubts and hopes of Guigemar, the lady's unspoken anguish, and the growing fear, resentment and jealousy of Meriadus. When the lovers are reunited the happy ending is still not complete, since the ungenerous Meriadus has to be disposed of, as are obstacles to happiness in other poems. Guigemar rapidly accomplishes this with the help of the forces of Meriadus's rival, thereby putting an end to the war at the same time. Although this may seem an unnecessary protraction of events, it does in fact show us the hero in yet another light, waging war on behalf of his lady as well as for his own glory.

Of all Marie's *lais*, *Guigemar* perhaps represents the most complete formulation of her modified courtly ethic, which is also successfully combined with elements of the Northern French tradition of chivalry. Unlike the standard situations in the Provençal lyric, the fact that the lady is married does not present the lovers with a serious obstacle. Rather it illustrates Marie's hostility towards an ill-matched couple and her sympathy for a pair she considers well-suited. Despite the early predominance of the supernatural in the *lai*, the otherworldly element remains strictly functional in bringing the lovers together in the first place so that their destiny may be fulfilled. For this reason *Guigemar* should not be seen as bearing any close resemblance to *Lanval*. There is no real evidence that Guigemar's lady is not of this world, although critics have made much of the comparison in line 704, 'Ke de beuté resemble fee'. On the other hand, both Guigemar and Lanval may be seen as characters who, for different reasons, are reserved for a special kind of love, one with a near perfect mortal, the other with a supernatural being. A closer similarity is probably to be found in *Eliduc*, where we shall see the same portrayal of *amour naissant*, this time in a young girl, but with a new complication, the conflict in the heart of the married man who loves her.

3 *The Dilemma of Choice:* Chaitivel *and* Eliduc

(i) *Two types of choice*

The *lai* of *Guigemar* followed Provençal courtly tradition in one very important aspect: the hero was not seen as having any freedom of choice. It was Guigemar's destiny to fall in love eventually, and when he did there was no question as to whom he should love. Similarly in the Provençal lyric, the merits of the courtly *dompna* require her suitor to love her and he is obliged to follow certain conventions in the hope of obtaining a reward. In the last chapter we saw how Marie de France expressed the whole courtly love tradition in her own terms, and we now have to consider the different facets of love and lovers that she selects for emphasis in the remaining eleven *lais*. The concept of choice is a convenient starting point, and in this chapter I shall try to show how it is examined from two very different points of view, resulting in two diametrically opposed solutions, in the *lais* of *Chaitivel* and *Eliduc*.

In these two poems two different types of choice are presented. In *Chaitivel* we have the story of a beautiful woman loved to excess by four equally worthy young knights, and the question of whom she should love is raised. The *lai* ends in tragedy because of the lady's irresolution and her uncourtly nature. In *Eliduc* the question is not whom to love, but whether to love at all. A happily married man, the epitome of courtliness, finds himself falling in love with a young girl, herself endowed with all the courtly virtues, and this time the problem can be resolved without tragedy only because of the supremely good nature of the third party, Eliduc's wife. Besides presenting two dilemmas, the *lais* complement each other in further respects. *Chaitivel* puts forward an extreme situation, so much so that it has often been seen as a parody of a love debate (the Provençal *razo*), where the problem would have been a familiar one to the medieval audience who have to answer the question: Who suffers most? If, however, we regard the *lai* as a genuine story, it seems that its main characteristic is, as Payen suggests (*40*, p. 324), a lack of courtly *mesure* on the part of the lady. By accepting the suits of all four knights she directly causes the death of three of them and the disablement of the fourth, and the outcome can only be grief, although how deeply this is felt by the lady is debatable. Eliduc, on the other hand, not only behaves with *mesure* in his relationship with his *amie*, but he does so in other aspects of his life as well, notably in the performance of his feudal duties and in his marriage. Consequently the *lai* ends on a note of joy, although the precise nature of this emotion is again open to debate.

In each *lai* a different concept of love prevails. *Chaitivel* sees it in the conventional terms of a reward granted to a faithful suitor. This view is shown to be untenable when there is no commitment on the part of the lady despite the merits of her potential lovers. She is incapable of experiencing loyalty, and in refusing to commit herself precipitates disaster. *Eliduc*, however, presents love in an altogether more elevated form. Not only are Eliduc and the girl Guilliadun an eminently suitable couple, in Marie's terms, but their commitment to each other is such that it leads to an even greater commitment to an ideal and ultimately divine love, firstly by Eliduc's wife Guildelüec and later by the couple themselves. The dilemmas of *Chaitivel* and *Eliduc* are both resolved, then, according to the nature of love, the one a base coquetry, the other a noble *fin'amors*.

In these *lais* very different character types are presented, which are good examples of the variety of Marie's heroes and heroines. The men in the two poems contrast strikingly. In *Chaitivel* they are young and inexperienced, seduced by the outward appearance of a beautiful woman without concern for her character defects. Their youthful overenthusiasm leads to tragedy, as does that of the boy in *Les deus amanz*. The surviving knight, however, matures through experience and displays a certain insight into the nature of the sorrow to which he is condemned and of the lady who has caused it. Eliduc, on the other hand, is a knight of prowess, like Guigemar, and a sensitive husband and committed lover. His love affair is described in terms analogous to those used of Tristan and Iseut in *Chevrefoil*.

The women in *Chaitivel* and *Eliduc* are also poles apart. The lady of *Chaitivel* shows little emotion other than self-pity, and must be ranked among those women regarded unfavourably by Marie, even though she does not display the spite and jealousy of the mother in *Le Fresne* or the criminal treachery of the wives in *Bisclavret* and *Equitan*. The predicament of a young girl falling in love for the first time is finely developed in *Eliduc*, and her hopes and fears are delicately and sympathetically conveyed. The compassion shown by Guildelüec is also a quality unequalled by Marie's other characters, with the possible exception of Fresne. Guildelüec is unique in that her love for her husband is surpassed only by her love for God, and it is significant that her abdication from her earthly marriage is eventually followed by a similar renunciation of this world by Eliduc and Guilliadun. In *Chaitivel* and *Eliduc*, then, two problems of choice are explored through different concepts of love and different types of character. In the one, an uncourtly lady has to choose between a number of worthy suitors, and her lack of choice leads to tragedy. In the other, a courtly knight has to decide between two ladies, and the nobility of all three characters demands an elevated spiritual conclusion. As we shall see, the *aventures* which are the subject of these complementary *lais* are vastly different.

(ii) *Chaitivel*

It is suggested at the end of *Chaitivel* that the interpretation of the poem hinges on the choice made between its alternative titles. This has led Sienaert (*45*, p. 147) to see the whole subject of the *lai* as 'la concurrence de deux titres', although this overlooks Marie's obvious preference for her own title. Nevertheless, a subject of debate is offered from the outset: are we concerned with one suffering knight or four? Marie's presentation of the problem (9-32) includes a general digression on the behaviour of courtly lovers, not unlike the digression on the nature of love in *Guigemar*, except that it is given a more prominent position. Its function is to help explain the significance of the *lai*, rather than to cover a gap in the narrative, as was the case in *Guigemar*. The introduction of the lady follows the pattern of several other accounts of uncourtly characters in Marie's poems, in that what is not said is more significant than the qualities directly ascribed to them. Thus we are told particularly of the lady's beauty (11, 31) and of her social rank and education (11-12), but she is not said to be either *curteise* or *sage* (cf. *Guigemar*, 212), and an equally telling omission occurs in *Bisclavret* (cf. lines 21-22).

As a result of her beauty the lady is widely admired and her dilemma, which is the true subject of the *lai*, is summed up in lines 17-18. Here Marie states a universal emotional problem, that of a woman who enjoys the flattery of men but who is reluctant to commit herself to just one. However, Marie states her own position quite clearly (the lady should honour those who serve her and not despise them) and she implicitly condemns her heroine before the details of the tragic outcome of the story are known. But, as in *Eliduc*, a common problem has to be worked out to its conclusion in terms of Marie's philosophy of love, and dramatic interest will not be lacking.

Like the lady herself, the four courtly suitors remain anonymous, which adds to the story's tone of a theoretical argument, but they are young. This is crucial in that they may be more readily deceived by the lady's beauty and apparent commitment, but they are also, by contrast, given the complete range of courtly epithets; besides being comely they are said to be 'pruz e vaillanz,/large, curteis e despendanz' (37-38). This last traditional feature of the courtly lover, his generosity, contrasts ironically with the apparent generosity of the lady which lies in her granting her love to all of them and which is really rooted in selfishness. Unlike his Provençal counterpart, the French courtly lover is, as I have already said, bound by additional ideals of chivalry, and the four knights here are characterized above all by the competitive spirit which prevails among them (42-48 and 61-66). Lines 49-58 describe the lady's behaviour in the face of this situation. There is a certain attempt on her part to make a choice, but no indication that her thoughts are particularly serious. Again it is a question of description by omission: there is no agony involved in the lady's appraisal of the situation, unlike that of Eliduc when torn between his wife and *amie*. Thus, not wishing to end up with one lover instead of four, the lady's solution is to encourage them all through her messages and love tokens. The effect of this description is, of course, to bind the knights to her service even more and to lead them to commit ever more daring deeds of chivalry in her name, with the rivalry between them necessarily continuing.

With the announcement of a tournament the lady is offered a last chance to make a decision, and, significantly, the four knights are referred to now as 'les quatre druz' (75, 85, 109). Their distinguishing feature of youthful rashness remains unchanged, as is evidenced by their unrestrained behaviour on the eve of the tournament. Thus, by the end of the first part of the *lai* (110) two forms of *démesure* have been established, one on the part of the lady, and the other on the part of the knights, and this continues throughout the rest of the action. When the tournament is over the young men prolong the fighting 'trop folement' (119) and the result of such extravagance is inevitably tragic. The lady's selfishness is seen in the contrast between the genuine grief of the assembled company for the dead knights and her lament for her own predicament, an opposition which is reflected in Marie's style. The description of mass sorrow is stressed through repetitions and superlatives, while the lady's speech is less extreme in its language and dominated by first person forms of unremarkable verbs. The emphasis here is placed firmly on her own feelings and her indecision as to whom is to be most pitied. Her actions in having the dead buried in style and the wounded knight well cared for reveal a concern for outward appearances as much as for the knights themselves, although there is no doubt as to where Marie's sympathies lie: 'Deus lur face bone merci!' (172).

The final section of the *lai*, almost a quarter of the length of the whole poem, deals with the facts of its composition, so that the creation of the *lai* itself becomes a significant theme. (By

contrast, the process of composition in *Chevrefoil* occupies only
the last 12 lines of the poem, about 10% of the whole.) It is
introduced as a distinct stage in the story through the change in
season (181) and the new situation where the lady and her
surviving admirer are alone together. For the first time the
young knight speaks, and there is a suggestion that his
experience has matured him. During the argument the lady
proclaims her intention of composing a *lai* specifically to
commemorate her own sorrow (202) and announces a title which
ranks all four knights together. With perhaps greater
psychological insight the survivor hastens to propose and justify
his own title (208), arguing that the suffering of his three
companions is over and that his is greater. In my own view the
anguish of the fourth knight is caused by his lady's continued
rejection of him because of her fickle nature, despite the loss of
the others (220-24). It must, however, be pointed out that critics
have more commonly attributed it to his castration (supposedly
indicated by lines 122-24), so that, ironically, the lady is left only
with a suitor who is no use to her. If this is so, then Marie is
unusually reticent on this crucial point. She has no qualms about
describing the condition of the eunuch priest in *Guigemar*, and
there is an equally explicit passage in the *Espurgatoire*. In either
case the knight's accusation is dramatic: 'Teus cent maus me
fetes suffrir' (223). Undoubtedly missing the significance of his
outburst the unrelenting lady consents immediately to the title of
Le Chaitivel ('ceo m'est bel' — 229), seeing the special pleading
as no more than her due.

Love, then ends in tragedy for the knights, but there is no
suggestion in *Chaitivel* that love is inherently tragic. It is the
démesure of the lady in encouraging all her suitors and of the
men in misplacing their attentions which causes the sad outcome
of the story. The problem of who suffers most remains
unsolved, although the implicit message is that death is to be
preferred to the suffering which is an inevitable consequence of
the fruitless pursuit of an uncourtly woman. As Payen has
pointed out (*40*, p. 325), there is no question of final repentance
or of love triumphant; instead we have 'le dénouement élégiaque
d'une tragédie qui s'achève sur la tendre tristesse d'une passion à

jamais insatisfaite et désespérée'.

(iii) *Eliduc*

The extreme situation depicted in *Chaitivel* has a more familiar counterpart in the *lai* of *Eliduc* where a husband's loyalty to his wife is overturned by his love for another woman. The *lai* is the story of his dilemma which, unlike that of *Chaitivel*, is resolved and does have a happy ending. The morality of *Chaitivel* hinged on the courtly concept of *mesure* in love, while that of *Eliduc* depends on a modification of Christian ethics, where the eternal triangle is resolved through sacrifice. Despite the increasing religious overtones, however, *Eliduc* does not adhere to Christian teaching on adultery. The basic moral problem is side-stepped by virtue of a certain oversimplification, and, according to De Caluwé (*16*, p. 76), Marie presents us with 'une conception de l'amour et du bonheur qui fait — ou voudrait faire — abstraction de toute loi morale'. While this is true, the end of the *lai* seems to be an attempt to portray the abstract courtly concept of *parfit'amur* in the concrete terms of religious life. Marie thus moves from the idealization of love proposed by secular troubadour poetry to a perfect love which transcends the problems of human relationships and can be attained only in the love of God. The Gospels teach that there is no marriage in heaven, and in making this the eventual message of the *lai* Marie has no hesitation in disregarding the moral teaching of the Church on earth. Eliduc's choice is, in a sense, made for him by the abdication of his wife in favour of his mistress, in much the same way as the lady in *Chaitivel* also has her theoretical problem solved by the natural course of events. But whereas the latter rejects the solution offered by fate and prolongs her indecision into death itself, Eliduc and Guilliadun accept Guildelüec's sacrifice and both ultimately reach Christian salvation, albeit by means of an apparently bigamous marriage.

Critics have differed as to the meaning and function of *Eliduc*. Hoepffner (*32*, ch. 9) saw it as having conjugal love as its distinctive feature, but this is tenable only insofar as this is the only *lai* in Marie's collection where love and loyalty between a married couple is given detailed consideration, and it is not, I think, at the centre of the *aventure*. Again it has been seen rather extravagantly as 'la perle du recueil' (Coppin *13*, p. 69), whereas Sienaert condemns somewhat harshly its narrative and psychological poverty (*45*, p. 165). I shall try to show through an analysis of the *lai* that it is in fact a moving and realistic portrayal of the dilemma as to whether and how to love. The eventual Christian outcome may, perhaps, be due to the subconscious guilt of the adulterous couple. This may be contrasted with the mysterious pagan Otherworld, which serves as a haven for Lanval and his fairy mistress.

Despite its unusual length, *Eliduc* has no more than a four-line prologue and epilogue, and follows the bi-partite structure of many of the shorter *lais*, although on a larger scale. The prologue mentions the *reisun* which Marie is giving to her story, which is reminiscent both of the *sen* referred to in the main Prologue and also of the conclusion of *Chaitivel* where the knight explains the *raisun* for his choice of title. The authenticity of the tale is also stressed (cf. line 28), while the epilogue emphasizes its commemorative function. It is worth bearing in mind that Marie uses the term *remembrance* for various purposes. In *Eliduc* the *lai* acts as a reminder of the three main characters and their relationship. In *Chaitivel* it was sorrow which was to be commemorated, while in *Chevrefoil* we shall see that the *lai* is used to preserve the message sent from Tristan to Iseut. When the protagonists are presented, Eliduc and his wife are introduced together and both are described in courtly terms. Here, as in *Guigemar*, the concept of loyalty is of supreme importance, since it will ultimately provide the salvation of all three characters. Guilliadun is introduced as a worthy rival to Guildelüec by virtue of her birth and beauty, although her courtliness has yet to be revealed.

(a) *Part I (29-549)*

Right from the outset different forms of loyalty are highlighted. Eliduc behaves *lëaument* in his service to his overlord (32), while there is the absence of *leauté* on the part of the latter, who accepts the word of slanderers against his vassal. Then Eliduc calls on the loyalty of friends to look after his wife in his absence. As Eliduc takes leave of his wife he promises 'Qu'il li porterat bone fei' (84), an oath of which we shall be reminded several times in the later love episode. In spite of Eliduc's sorrow at leaving home his immediate instinct is to seek adventure, and the interaction of chivalrous and courtly themes is particularly evident in this *lai*, where an almost epic battle scene, provoked by the dispute as to Guilliadun's future, precedes the main action. Eliduc's speech to his men (185-200) has unmistakable epic overtones and his promise of commitment to his men is couched in feudal terms (186). In his campaign Eliduc is shown to be successful as a leader and also personally outstanding (249), by which time the preparations for his relationship with the king's daughter are near completion.

The second half of part I begins on a note of total contrast (271). With the prospect of lasting peace the pace becomes slower and tentative feelings replace decisive events. The new subject matter is introduced by a reminder of Eliduc's courtly qualities, but for the first time he is described as *beau* (272). Similarly Guilliadun's beauty is recalled (294) and, as in *Guigemar* (453), the future compatibility of the couple is suggested. Their first meeting is characterized by extreme politeness and propriety and Eliduc, seen through Guilliadun's eyes, is altogether gentler in his manner, as his comeliness is restated in more detail (301-2). His attraction for her is expressed in Ovidian terms (304-5) and the immediate effect is two-fold: a physical reaction (*palir, suspirer* (306)) and an emotional reaction of fear (308), a feeling which dominates the girl's nascent love. She is afraid of two things: firstly rejection, then, later, an alliance with a man about whom she knows nothing. It is clear from line 315 that Eliduc is also attracted to her, but his thoughts are halted by the memory of his wife. We are reminded of their continuing commitment in marriage by the feudal terminology already used in this context (cf. line 84), *bone fei, lëaument* (325-26), and this intrusive thought recurs at subsequent stages in the development of the love between Eliduc and Guilliadun.

From line 327 Guilliadun's feelings and intentions are made

increasingly explicit. First her desire is obvious (328), then her
love (339) and finally her willingness for a physical relationship
(345) with its attendant suggestion of marriage (347), all of
which culminates in her association of unrequited love and death
(349-50). Guilliadun initiates the action of using her
chamberlenc as an advisor, and the theme of loyalty occurs
again: 'Li ad duné conseil leal' (353). Having dispatched tokens
of her feelings to Eliduc, the heroine's fate is in the balance. Her
dilemma, as to whether her actions will lead to happiness or folly
depending on the courtliness of Eliduc, is the converse of the
lady's problem in *Chaitivel*, and anticipates Eliduc's hesitancy in
making his own choice.

At line 401 the interest turns to Eliduc's reactions. His silent
donning of Guilliadun's gifts suggests acceptance of her love,
and it is significant that the messenger's main impression of him
is his discretion (424) and that he is not *jolis* (422) (fickleness
being a short-coming equally disliked by the *trobairitz*). The
feudal motif recurs with the sudden revelation that Eliduc is to
be retained for a year in loyal service to the king, which has the
effect of replacing Guilliadun's doubts by joy. This contrasts
with Eliduc's sorrow as he wrestles with his conscience and
remembers his promise of *lëauté* to his wife (467) and of keeping
faith both with her and the king (475-76). In spite of the
different emotions of the couple, however, Eliduc who, already
dreams of loving Guilliadun (471-72), is committing adultery in
his heart. Once Marie has indicated their mutual love the couple
reveal their feelings to each other, which are at first delicately
expressed in free indirect speech (507-18), then in a joyful
outburst of direct speech. The establishing of a courtly
relationship is completed through the courtly vocabulary of
Guilliadun's reply and Marie's summary at the end of the first
part of the *lai*.

(b) *Part II (550-1180)*

The second half of the *lai* deals with the consequences of the love
described in the first half. The couple's separation is followed by
a reunion which is apparently disastrous until the dilemma of
choice posed by the poem is resolved. The intermingling of

chivalrous and courtly episodes is again reflected in corresponding changes of speed in the narrative. Thus Eliduc's summons to come home and the explanation of the treachery which originally forced him to leave is rapidly conveyed in 20 lines (550-70) with a renewed used of feudal terms, *aliance* (567) and *umage* (568), to remind us of his obligations in this respect. Lines 571-618, by contrast, move slowly, giving Eliduc's reaction to this request and his feelings for Guilliadun, with his monologue revealing his divided loyalties. It is clearly stated (575-76) that technically adultery has not taken place: their love is romantic rather than sexual, and this leads Marie to limit the meaning of *drüerie* to romantic courtship (579), discarding its usual overtones of uncourtly physical love, which it has, for example, in *Equitan* (15). The innocence of the lovers is restated later when Guilliadun is consistently referred to as *pucele* (746 and 1012). Her hope is, of course, to marry Eliduc and we are reminded of her ignorance of his marriage: 'Ne saveit pas que femme eüst' (584).

Eliduc's monologue is one of remorse reflecting a complex situation. He states his various obligations: his love for Guilliadun (588), his loyalty to his wife (597) and to God (602), and his feudal duty (611). He admits his sin in terms which contain a hint of possible *démesure*: 'Mal ai erré!/Trop ai en cest païs esté!' (585-86) and expresses his regret hyperbolically: 'Mar vi unkes ceste cuntree!' (587). Indeed, Eliduc's behaviour epitomises divided loyalties, for in telling the king he will return if necessary he is committing himself to serving two masters as well as two women (cf. his 'loyal' promise to Guilliadun in line 690 to return). His leave-taking from Guilliadun is delicately portrayed as the girl's joy at seeing him turns rapidly to acute distress. Such sorrow grieves Eliduc — a further indication of the genuine nature of their love — and culminates in his declaration of total commitment, reminiscent of that found in Thomas's *Tristan* (*48*, pp. 74 and 144):

> Vus estes ma vie e ma mort
> En vus est [tres]tut mon confort! (671-72)

After Eliduc has taken leave of his lady in accordance with chivalrous convention his journey home is swift and easy, like the voyages in *Guigemar*, but in striking contrast to the one that is to come. This contrast is echoed in that between the general rejoicing at the hero's return and Eliduc's own grief (715-16). Eliduc excuses himself by explaining his pledge to his new overlord and his promise to return in due course, omitting that made to the king's daughter, although line 739, 'ne voil ma fei trespasser', is ambiguous. Spurred on by his time limit Eliduc manages to achieve his task of making peace and prepares for his return voyage by carefully selecting his companions and swearing them to secrecy, which leaves us in little doubt as to what is to follow.

Marie offers no explanation for Eliduc's apparent change of heart in bringing Guilliadun home with him, beyond the fact that the time limit set by her has expired and that he is behaving in a truly courtly manner: 'Bien ad sun cuvenant tenu' (770). Now, however, the theme of secrecy is developed and Eliduc is described as cunning, *veizïez* (763). Two details in the passage 759-98 have struck some critics as suggestive of a female author. In line 775 we are told that the *chamberlenc* has changed his clothes before attempting to see Guilliadun and in lines 796-98 we have details of the girl's clothing at the time of her elopement. However, the significance of these details is perhaps more than feminine observation, for they are indicative of the girl's noble birth and her beauty, which will move the heart of Guildelüec when she first sees her. The lovers' reunion is marked by a change of mood in Guilliadun , which is the reverse of that which we saw at their parting: 'De joie plure tendrement' (785) and there is no condemnation by Marie of the deception which Eliduc is practising in this operation.

The crucial importance of the storm episode (815ff.) is conveyed by the amount of detail Marie uses in its description, which culminates in the outburst of a sailor who fears for his life. His speech reflects the ancient belief that the presence of a wrongdoer on board ship provokes the wrath of God (cf. the Old Testament story of Jonah), and the sailor's solution is that Guilliadun should be thrown overboard in appeasement (840). It is interesting that Eliduc, their master, is not seen as the guilty party, although he has betrayed his 'femme leale' (835) and has disobeyed the laws of God and man. But while this somewhat rhetorical speech is a realistic expression of the mood of the company, its primary function is to reveal to Guilliadun the fact of Eliduc's marriage. Eliduc's response is to threaten the sailor with dire consequences (845-46), a threat which he does indeed carry out when it appears that Guilliadun has died of the shock. His anger is conveyed in unusually strong language, which is indicative of the gravity of the offence committed against love as Marie sees it.

Thus, despite Eliduc's attempts at comforting her (for her seasickness as well as for her emotional plight), Guilliadun seems to fall into a coma, so that in line 858 there is the first of several statements that she is taken for dead (cf. 872 and 934). Punishment is then inflicted on the sailor, an act seen by Fitz (*22*) as a necessary and logical sacrifice in place of Guilliadun, since he seems to think that all those on board share Eliduc's guilt. Eliduc himself brings the ship safely to port, an act of heroism and skill which is played down in the face of the lovers' crisis. With Eliduc now expressing a death wish (874) we are constantly reminded of death and sorrow. As his thoughts turn to a fitting burial and monument for Guilliadun, both as his beloved and as a princess, the religious theme which characterizes the poem's dénouement becomes increasingly evident. Eliduc's lament (938-50) bewails the fatal nature of their love, which he sees as 'amur leale e fine' (944); she has loved him *lëaument* (945) and all he can do now is to turn to the religious life. Thus, as far as Eliduc is concerned, the loss of his beloved must lead him to elevate his passion onto a spiritual plane, rather than to return to his wife.

The last section of the *lai* restates the basic problem in slightly different terms: Eliduc is now caught in a dilemma between continuing with his earthly marriage or devoting himself to the memory of his apparently dead *amie*. The dilemma begins to be resolved with Guildelüec's discovery of Guilliadun, which also provides Marie with an opportunity for describing the girl objectively (1012-16). Guildelüec at once understands the implications of what she has found: 'Ceo est l'amie mun seigneur' (1023). Such is her generosity, both towards her husband and the girl that, moved by the latter's beauty, she herself is led to intense grief (1028-31). Then follows the curious incident of the weasel, an animal traditionally associated with various magical powers, but the supernatural element is here firmly set in a Christian context. The animal appears from beneath the altar and is killed by the *vadlet* because it ran across Guilliadun's body, defiling it (1035). When its mate appears and attempts to revive it, Marie does not indulge in a medieval version of the pathetic fallacy, but simply tells us that the animal seems to be displaying sorrow. The flower which the weasel uses to bring its companion back to life is recognized by Guildelüec as having life-giving properties, and thus by virtue of such quick thinking Guilliadun is awakened. A further indication of Guildelüec's character comes in her immediate prayer of thanksgiving (1068).

The ensuing conversation between the two women is a good representation of their respective characters. Guilliadun, having been betrayed, as she had feared, by the man she loves, reverts to her former scepticism (cf. 308), 'Mut est fole quë humme creit' (1084), while Guildelüec seeks to comfort her by telling her of her husband's extreme grief and her own similar emotions. She concludes with the ultimate act of love, taking Guilliadun to her husband and promising to renounce the world and take the veil. Such generosity does not pass unremarked by Eliduc in the midst of his joy at his beloved's return: 'Ducement sa femme mercie' (1114). Equally, Guildelüec recognizes true love in their *semblant* (1120) and in an elevated form of the courtly ethic seeks *congé* of her husband to leave him to serve God. The legality of the situation is questionable; Eliduc gives his wife a portion of his land to build a convent on the site where he had originally intended to commemorate Guilliadun. There is no reference to any official annulment of the marriage, but events move swiftly as the convent is built, a religious order established and Eliduc marries Guilliadun. Their marriage is characterized by *parfit'amur* (1150) and both, through their generosity and good works, are led eventually also to commit their lives to God, and found a church and an order of monks. Religious lines dominate the ending (1164, 1169, 1180), in which Guildelüec receives her husband's second wife into the convent and instructs her (1170). Thus it is eventually possible for Eliduc and his two wives to be united in their love for one another as they turn their energies to their individual love for God. Perfect love between each couple in turn is shown to lead to spiritual perfection, and it is fitting that Marie's epilogue should commemorate the story of all three characters rather than just one.

As with the lady in *Chaitivel*, it does seem for a while that Eliduc is able to enjoy the best of all worlds. But whereas the former, through lack of courtly love, could not make her choice even when the dilemma was resolved for her, Eliduc and his wives, all courtly characters, remove the original need for a choice at all. The dilemma is resolved on one level by the abdication of Guildelüec and on another by the union of all three in a perfect love which transcends any earthly ideal.

4 *Obstacles to Love:* Equitan, Le Fresne, Milun

In the last chapter I tried to show how the question of choice and its resolution may be seen as central to the plot of *Eliduc* and *Chaitivel*. Similarly here, I should like to consider three *lais*, *Equitan*, *Le Fresne* and *Milun*, as being based above all on a single idea, that of love being in some way obstructed. Clearly this was also a theme in *Eliduc*, insofar as Eliduc's marriage might be seen as an obstacle to his liaison with Guilliadun, but it is not the only preoccupation of the *lai*. In the three *lais* to be discussed here, however, obstacles which threaten or, in the case of *Milun*, demand the separation of the couple are of paramount importance. In each case it is possible to see these obstacles as being of a social rather than of a moral or physical nature.

Although all three *lais* appear to share this motif of a social obstacle, *Equitan* stands in contrast to the other two. In *Equitan* the love affair is between two characters of unequal social standing and their love is further hindered by the fact that the lady is already married and that Equitan (like Fresne's lover) comes under pressure to marry. Their way of overcoming these two obstacles to their adulterous relationship is to resort to criminal action, which is wholeheartedly condemned by Marie, whose sympathy this time obviously does not lie with the lovers. In both *Le Fresne* and *Milun*, on the other hand, as in other *lais*, Marie appears to look favourably upon the lovers' extra- or premarital physical relationships, although she is critical of adultery as it is portrayed in *Equitan*. The solution to the problems posed in *Le Fresne* and *Milun* is one of passive fidelity, and it is this which is rewarded by the eventual reunion of the lovers. In *Le Fresne* the obstacle to love is the pressure to marry exerted on the lover, together with the unknown social class of the girl herself, while in *Milun* it is the lady who is forced to marry in her lover's absence. So in both *lais* a social obstacle is overcome by patience and fidelity, but in *Equitan* criminal action tragically fails to remove the barrier to adulterous love. These three *lais* contrast in turn with *Les deus amanz* and *Chevrefoil* and even *Laüstic*, where it is a physical obstacle which has to be overcome if the couples are to be brought together at all, but where, in any case, tragedy is the dominant theme.

(i) *Equitan*

In *Equitan* Marie seems to be using her source material to demonstrate the impracticability of the courtly concept of the superiority of the lady, as formulated by the Provençal troubadours, when it is worked out in depth, which is the same technique that she has already used in *Chaitivel*. The traditionally adulterous nature of courtly love is shown to be destructive when it is accompanied by *démesure*, a failing which is clearly exemplified in the lovers' inability to control their passion at the very point where the obstacle to it is about to be removed, and the gruesome fate which befalls them in consequence. This flaw in the characters of both Equitan and his mistress becomes apparent very early in the *lai* and as a result events move swiftly and relentlessly towards the inevitable conclusion. It is significant, therefore, that when Equitan is first introduced he is described as *curteis* (11), but adjectives normally associated with this epithet are reserved for the seneschal who is 'Bon chevaler, pruz e leal' (22). It is also worth bearing in mind the feudal origins of some of the terminology of courtliness, since this is a *lai* where an uncourtly love affair risks jeopardizing the social order. The significance of Equitan's weakness, his fondness for *deduit* and *druerie* (16), is stressed by one of Marie's short interventions (17-20) which emphasizes in general terms the importance of 'sen e mesure' in love. When the seneschal is presented, on the other hand, he, like Marie's other courtly characters, is said to be *leal* (22), and this feudal and marital loyalty will contrast forcefully with the absence of such a quality in his wife.

Marie's introduction of the seneschal's wife leaves us in no more doubt as to her destructive role in the story: 'Dunt puis vient el païs granz mal[s]' (30), than did the presentation of Equitan. As with the lady in *Chaitivel* the description centres on outward appearances rather than on internal qualities, and lines 31-37 constitute a miniature portrait of her beauty, culminating in the superlative 'El rëaume n'aveit sa per' (37). It is the lack of any further description which is again suggestive of uncourtliness. In *Eliduc*, by contrast, the presentation of Guilliadun in terms of her beauty was further enhanced by her modest behaviour that followed. Like Guilliadun, Equitan is attracted to his partner by her reputation, but whereas the courtly Guilliadun invited her future lover to 'esbanïer/E parler e bien acuinter' (*Eliduc*, 277-78), Equitan in fact covets his seneschal's wife (41) and seeks to amuse himself with her privately, 'Priveement esbanïer' (43), so that from the outset she is associated with his 'deduit'. In Equitan's eyes the lady is clearly worthy of his love (51-52), although this view is not necessarily shared by Marie. The Ovidian metaphor of love's arrow is again used, with the result that Equitan becomes 'murnes e pensis' (60) (cf. *Eliduc*, 314) and, like Marie's other lovers, sleepless. His insomnia leads naturally into a long monologue (65-88) in which his physical longing is linked with his awareness of its wrongfulness. His moral misgivings appear to be based on the feudal loyalty between himself and his seneschal: 'Garder li dei amur e fei/Si cum jeo voil k'il face a mei' (73-74), and at least a fleeting concern for his feelings, 'mut l'en pesereit' (76). Such reservations are, however, quickly overcome by the thought that the lady needs a lover to preserve her 'curteisie' (!), and therefore her husband ought not to be too worried by possible rumours: 'Ne l'en deit mie trop peser' (86). Thus, by means of a specious argument, Equitan allows his self-interest to prevail and his monologue (91-100) creates a further contrast with the *amour naissant* of Eliduc and Guilliadun, in that there is here little genuine debate and self-questioning.

The love affair that ensues is characterized throughout by deception and disloyalty. The train of events begins with a hunting motif (103), but, unlike its occurrence in Arthurian Romance, or even in *Guigemar*, this leads not to chivalrous adventure but to disastrous sexual intrigue, a neat illustration of

Marie's technique of creating variations on well-established themes. When Equitan declares his love, it is the lady who brings up the subject of the social difference between them, the question of adultery not, apparently, being taken into account. This again enables Marie to put a generalization about the nature of love into the mouth of her character (cf. *Guigemar*, 483, 'Amurs est plai...'), stating that love is only *pruz* when it is between equals. Perhaps the seneschal's wife recognizes something of Equitan's character, for the idea of loyalty occurs several times (138 and 142) and is specifically linked with happiness (*joie*) in love (140-42). It is, however, equally possible that Marie is presenting her as hoping for a promise of social or financial privilege. Certainly she seems to equate the difference between them with wealth (122, 138, 144, 146) rather than status, which is echoed by the fact that her husband acts as a replacement for Equitan at court, while Equitan's reply is to criticize a 'bourgeois' trust in material possessions (152-54). He proceeds to suggest that courtliness resides instead in one's attitude to love: a woman who sets a high price on her lover and is not fickle, if she is 'sage,/curteise e franche de curage' (155-56) will inspire love in the richest of princes. This does not quite coincide with the Provençal concept of courtliness where the lady is traditionally of more noble birth than her lover, although Marie does use a rather basic image found also in the earliest troubadour Guillaume IX ('sul son mantel', 159), who does not always coincide with later convention. Equitan does, however, purport to share the ideal of 'lealment e bien amer' (162) and he condemns unfaithful lovers, while encouraging a woman to deceive a good husband. The courtly tradition of the lover's abasement before his lady is pushed to the extreme, as the king urges her to forget his high position, and Marie seems to be condemning the excesses of courtly convention in his suggestion: 'Vus orguilluse e jeo preiant' (176), quite apart from censuring the implicit *démesure* of line 175 (cf. lines 17 and 237). Certainly she immediately anticipates and emphasizes the disastrous outcome with her synonyms 'en mururent e finerent' (184).

This tragedy is initiated by Equitan's refusal to seek a wife elsewhere, which does indeed indicate a certain loyalty to his mistress. The lady's plot to free herself from her husband and thus to overcome this obstacle to her love affair begins with a display of feminine guile similar to that found in *Bisclavret*. She chooses the moment of love-making to reveal her fears that Equitan will take a wife who is his social equal (215), with the frequency of the first person in this lament echoing the self-centred speeches of the lady in *Chaitivel*. Her reference to love causing her own death (219) is as fleeting and unconvincing as that already expressed by Equitan (174), but it does have the important function of leading Equitan to contemplate his seneschal's death and of provoking his rash promise:

> Si vostres sire fust finez,
> Reïne e dame vus fereie. (226-27)

Equitan is equally foolish in submitting to the most outrageous demands of his lady before hearing them, and the plan which she puts forward must surely be preconceived. As the plot is put into effect, Marie twice reminds us that evil rebounds on its instigator (299, 310). While the fatal bath is being prepared we are told, with a touch of realism, that the seneschal goes for a walk to pass the time (278), and this is the point at which the couple's *démesure* is fully revealed. In Marie's account of the discovery of the guilty pair there is, perhaps, a hint of black humour in the detail that one goes to his death feet first, while the wife is thrown head first into the boiling water, which might be suggestive of the disparity which has existed throughout between the guilty couple.

Although the outcome of this *lai* is a tragic one, it is the idea of guilt which is emphasized above all, and Marie obviously intended her tale to have a moral function (308-10). Through their impatience and evil action the couple have failed to resolve the problem of their love, and as the antithesis of the modified courtly doctrine which she advocates, *Equitan* has an important function within Marie's collection. I cannot agree with Wind that this is simply the story of 'un amour bassement adultère sans aucun des raffinements qui rachètent l'infidélité dans l'amour courtois' (*51*, p. 743).

(ii) *Le Fresne*

Whereas *Equitan* treated the removal of a social obstacle to an adulterous relationship which was disastrous because of the fault of *démesure*, both *Le Fresne* and *Milun* are concerned initially with a pre-marital relationship, the social obstacles to which are eventually overcome successfully because of the *mesure* of one or both lovers. Both these two *lais* contain a new element, that of children, although their function in each is quite different. The social pressure to marry, resisted by Equitan, is accepted by Fresne's lover and Milun's mistress. In *Le Fresne* the girl's sacrifice leads to a rapid annulment of the marriage, but in *Milun* the couple cannot be reunited until their son is of an age to perform the necessary task. *Le Fresne* is the only *lai* in the collection to take its title from the name of the heroine and is, in effect, a character study of the girl, and, to a lesser extent, of her mother. It could, perhaps, be argued that there is a cyclical movement to the poem, which begins and ends with the concept of the family and its growth. The obstacle to the couple's love is a social and economic objection raised by Gurun's liegemen, and this is satisfactorily resolved by the revelation of the girl's origins and her reunion with her family, thanks to Fresne's character and moderate behaviour throughout the story.

The courtliness of Fresne's background is shown particularly in the figure of her father, whose courtly behaviour is seen both in his rebuke of his wife's slandering and, most notably, at the end of the *lai* when he is reunited with a daughter of whose very existence he had hitherto been ignorant. The separation of the heroine from her family is brought about by the use of a common folklore theme, the idea that the birth of twins results from intercourse with two men. However, Marie, as we might expect, uses this motif for her own purposes, to pinpoint the uncourtly jealousy of Fresne's mother when twin boys are born to her neighbour, and to provide an example of natural justice when she herself, by a rather bizarre coincidence, gives birth to twin girls. When this happens the mother's first instincts are murderous (which is reminiscent of the lady in *Equitan*), but Marie suggests that the woman does have some redeeming features, for she is well-liked and well-served by her attendants, one of whom plays an important part in the story by disposing of the unwanted child. The faithful servant to whom the baby is entrusted is herself of noble birth (100) and through her a religious strain enters the tale, which is never completely absent. The baby's immediate welfare (at the convent in a rich town) depends on a second coincidence, that the porter's daughter is already a nursing mother, and the fact that she is a widow provides a convenient explanation of how she comes to be living with her father. The orders given by her father (201-2) might be indicative of Marie's own awareness of childcare, and similar details are to be found in the parallel situation in *Milun* (11-12). At this point the emblems of the ring and the coverlet which the baby has been given by her mother fulfil their first function, in providing evidence of her noble birth. This is perhaps also recognized by the abbess who makes what must have been an unusual decision, to bring up the child as her own niece.

Fresne's lover, Gurun, behaves in accordance with the courtly ethic of some of the troubadours in that he falls in love with the girl without having seen her (247-48), and he devises a means of seeing her more often by making a gift of land to the convent, which gives him the right of 'repaire e ... sejur' (266). This particular custom is examined by Nagel (*38*, p. 456), who points out that in making this gift Gurun is clearly not thinking of the good of his soul, as Marie indeed suggests (266-70). His proposal that he and Fresne elope suggests that Fresne would otherwise be destined for the religious life. After this, however, Gurun becomes a rather more passive character, which allows Fresne's nature to be highlighted accordingly. He agrees to the argument put forward by his liegemen who, understandably, in feudal terms, put pressure on him to marry and produce an heir, and he accepts their preference for Codre. The names of the girls can only be symbolic and this enables Marie to make a pun about the fruitfulness as well as the delight of the hazel in contrast to the ash, although admittedly the parallel is rather forced. Marie in no way appears to be criticizing the action of the knights, but is only regretful that they are acting in ignorance, hence her interjection (345-50), which also serves to inform her audience, if they have not already guessed, that Codre is indeed Fresne's twin sister.

Emotions predominate towards the end of the *lai*. Above all, Fresne's generosity prevails, amid the sorrow of the household at losing her. Then, in contrast, there is the hostility and fear of her mother in dealing with the obviously well-known relationship between Fresne and Gurun, although this fear is dispelled by Fresne's modest behaviour at the marriage. The ring and the coverlet reappear with a new function, that of allowing the mother to recognize her daughter, while the coverlet also symbolises the sacrifices, both material and emotional, which Fresne is prepared to make for her lover. At the moment of Fresne's mother's revelation of her daughter's identity the father reappears on the scene and his courtly character, noted already at the beginning, is shown in his concern for his wife and his readiness to pardon her as yet unconfessed fault. His reaction is one of sheer joy at the news of '*nostre* fille' (479, 487) and thanksgiving that a further crime has been averted (489), and his sentiments are echoed in the happiness of Fresne and Gurun. With the initial objection to the lack of dowry now overcome the loose ends of the story are quickly tied up. In conclusion we are told of Codre's successful marriage elsewhere and of the naming of the *lai* after its heroine. This name is by now rich in symbolic meaning, indicating first the foundling child and secondly complete compliance. The outcome is a happy one as selfless and faithful love triumphs both in the union of marriage and the reuniting of a family.

(iii) *Milun*

The *lai* of *Milun* complements *Fresne* in a variety of ways. Both have the theme of faithful love being rewarded, although this is not the dominant element in either poem, and this loyalty is established through a pre-marital relationship condoned by the author. Fidelity enables the lovers to transcend certain obstacles, namely the marriage of the lady in *Milun* and the un-consummated marriage of the knight in *Fresne*. In each case the recognition between parent and child has important consequences for the pairs of lovers who are thus seen not in isolation but in a wider set of relationships. Both stories are precipitated by a fear of gossip on the part of the mothers of unwanted babies, and coincidence also plays a role in each (in *Milun* it is the convenient death of the husband). In both *lais* love begins before the couple have even met, once on the part of the knight (*Le Fresne*) and once on the part of the lady (*Milun*). Both stories contain recognition devices to reunite parents and children, and in both the traditional ring is supplemented by something else. The bedcover in *Le Fresne* symbolizes more than faithful love, and the swan in *Milun* is the means by which loyal contact is maintained. Structurally the *lais* closely resemble each other, with love being established and an obstacle introduced in the first half, and the reunion of the lovers resulting from the recognition of parent and child in the second half. In both, an extra character has to be removed: husband in *Milun* and the sister in *Le Fresne*.

The lovers in *Milun* are clearly compatible, Milun being credited with courtly qualities in addition to his considerable prowess. The girl is described as *bele* and *mut curteis* (23-24), which subsumes all the necessary qualities, and each is said to be joyful, *liez* (29, 47), at the interest of the other. Their love is to be secret, although for no very obvious reason, and in true courtly fashion Milun pledges himself to come at her bidding (41-42). However, the courtly element is greatly reduced and, more realistically, the lovers' union being shown to be a physical one, we are brought rapidly to the central interest of the introductory passages, the lady's pregnancy and its consequences. The separation of the baby from its parents is, of course, analogous to the scene in *Le Fresne*, but has a different motivation, that of a social stigma with possibly horrific consequences, rather than mere gossip. We see that while pre-marital sexual relations may have been condoned in the society of which Marie writes, illegitimate births certainly are not, and she refers to a particularly repulsive treatment of expectant mothers 'en cel tens' (64). Thus arrangements for disposing of the child, this time with no evil intent, are made before its birth, but as in *Le Fresne* the baby is to take a ring with it, along with explicit (rather than implicit) details of the circumstances of its birth and instructions to seek out its father in due course.

The child's departure is followed by the separation of the lovers themselves: the obstacle to their happiness. Milun is required to set out in search of fame as a knight, while his mistress is forcibly married to a man who has none of the traditional courtly characteristics (127-28). The lady's fears when confronted with the prospect of such a husband, who will realise that she is not a virgin, are apparently well-founded, for after her marriage she seems to be virtually imprisoned by her husband. The lovers' future communication is by the unusual means of a swan. The significance of the swan is fully discussed by C. Bullock-Davies (7), who suggests that it is part of an identifiable background in South Wales where there was a natural breeding ground for swans; this implies that Marie is introducing realistic details into her story at the same time as creating a variant on the literary convention of a bird or human messenger. Bullock-Davies takes a somewhat prosaic view of the correspondence that follows, describing the swan as 'only a postman' who 'does nothing but carry secret letters between an ageing hero and his lady-love for the unromantic length of twenty years' (7, p. 21). Yet, on the other hand, one might well see in the bird's beauty a very romantic symbol of faithful love which eventually finds its own reward. The patience displayed by the couple while their son grows up is a reflection, on a larger time-scale, of the restraint of Fresne as she watches her lover prepare to marry someone else.

From line 291 the main subject of the rest of the *lai* is Milun's son, who grows up to rival his father in courtliness and knightly prowess. The young man achieves a courtly reputation through his valour and generosity (*largesse* being generally held to be important in courtly literature, cf. also *Lanval* and *Guigemar*) and this eventually reaches the ears of his father. Milun, being a typically chivalrous knight, is upset at the news of a new Knight Peerless, to the extent that the idea becomes something of an obsession with him. Thus the son is made a worthy opponent of and successor to his father, and Milun is given the necessary motivation to meet him. Although Milun has a long-standing reputation as a knight, it is only in the final tournament that his military skills are exploited in the *lai*, just as those of Guigemar were only worthy of interest in his efforts to regain his lost mistress.

The tournament scene at the end is reminiscent of that portrayed in *Chaitivel*, with its enumeration of the different nationalities represented, but it is also significant that the British are few in number, and therefore Milun and his son will have little difficulty in encountering each other. Marie gives us a brief insight into the organization of an event where everyone could be expected to meet his match, and tells us of Milun's short-lived success (406). The revelation of the identity of father and son is given a thoroughly realistic setting, with Milun catching sight of his ring on his son's hand as the latter gallantly helps him to his feet. The reunion that follows illustrates Marie's ability to portray moving situations, as she expounds each detail, ending with the boy's determination to reunite his parents himself, by removing the obstacle of his mother's tyrannical husband.

Thus father and son return home together, only to find a message telling them of the death of the husband, a coincidence which prevents any possible *démesure* in the form of criminal behaviour from entering the story. With the obstacle to their love already removed, the son nonetheless performs a ritual of reuniting his parents, who live happily ever after, a story with which Marie says she is well content (536). As in *Le Fresne*, the theme of the family is given particular prominence at the end of the *lai* and reinforces the conclusion that faithful and innocent love (in Marie's terms) will be duly rewarded, whereas any uncourtly criminal and immoderate action to remove an obstacle, as in *Equitan*, is unequivocally condemned.

5 *Love and the Supernatural:* Lanval, Yonec, Bisclavret

(i) *The supernatural provides love:* Lanval *and* Yonec

The previous chapter has provided us with three instances in which an established love affair has had to overcome social obstacles, and *Lanval* and *Yonec* offer a further variation on this theme. In these two *lais* a love intrigue is presented initially as a means of combating a social injustice. In each case the protagonist is socially isolated, either through loneliness and injustice from his peers (*Lanval*), or through mismarriage to an elderly husband (*Yonec*), and by a judicious use of the supernatural, Marie provides an answer to an apparently insuperable problem before developing its consequences. This technique, has, of course, already been seen in *Guigemar*, where a magic boat enabled the lovers to meet, but there the supernatural was little more than incidental to the main theme of the love between two mortals. In *Lanval* and *Yonec* on the other hand, and also in *Bisclavret*, supernatural elements play a key role in the stories, which deal for the most part with the love between a mortal and a supernatural being. The first two *lais* are to a certain extent complementary. In *Lanval* the supernatural being is a fairy and the lover is a mortal, whereas in *Yonec* a mortal lady is loved by a fairy prince. In the former there is no adultery, while in the latter the adulterous relationship is, in Marie's eyes, excusable. Both poems present more forcefully than hitherto the concept of *démesure*, a fault to which the mortal in each case succumbs. In *Lanval* this results in the temporary withdrawal of the fairy's love for the hero, although the lovers are eventually reunited in the Other World. In *Yonec* the consequences are tragic; again the mortal is deprived of love, but this time permanently, in earthly terms, until the couple's eventual reunion in death. Different forms of *démesure* which also have a tragic outcome will be discussed in the next chapter with reference to *Les deus amanz* and *Laüstic*, but the outstanding characteristic of both *Lanval* and *Yonec* is the excessive love of the mortal partner for the other, rather than the tragic atmosphere which marks the two shorter *lais*. Thus *Lanval* and *Yonec* have a similar thematic structure in which the supernatural provides love which is subsequently withdrawn, because of some *démesure* on the part of the mortal, only to be restored or avenged in conclusion. At the end of each *lai* the real and supernatural worlds appear to be fused, and, despite the importance of the Other World, realistic elements predominate throughout.

(a) *Lanval*

The structure of *Lanval* is a tripartite one. Firstly we see a supernatural being giving her love to a mortal who is sworn to secrecy (39-218); secondly, as a result of Lanval's weakness, that love is withdrawn and a judicial trial in earthly terms ensues as well (237-470); thirdly, the long dénouement shows the resolution of the trial through the restoration of the fairy's love and the departure of the couple from the real world to Avalon. Initially, the adventure is set in traditional terms by the reference to Pentecost (11), and Arthur's court is evoked by the use of superlatives which stress above all its richness. In contrast we have Lanval who is courtly (21-22, 27), but who is inexplicably overlooked in the king's distribution of wealth to his knights. Like Fresne he accepts his lot without complaint, and remains alone and sorrowful in a foreign court. Much has been made of the fact that Marie has great sympathy for the plight of a stranger (33-34, 37), with some critics emphasizing a possible parallel with Marie herself, a Frenchwoman in England, and some stressing Lanval's 'otherness' which renders him suitable for an encounter with a being from the Other World. The renown of Arthur's court is perhaps somewhat tarnished by the events recounted, and the court becomes in the course of the *lai* symbolic of temporal, as opposed to supernatural, justice.

The appearance of the supernatural is anticipated by three details: the hero's physical distance from normal life (43), the proximity of water (45) and the inexplicable fear of Lanval's horse (46). As we have already seen in *Guigemar*, the Other World is characterized by its incomparable richness, and here the servants are described in terms of their superlative beauty and the magnificence of their dress. The literal significance of the basin and towel which they bear is not apparent until later (178-79), but already they are symbolic of some initiation rite which also suggest entry into another world. It is also possible that the fairy is meeting Lanval at a point between two worlds, since her speech emphasizes the fact that she has left her own land for him.

The lovers address each other in the language of courtly tradition, and the fairy asks only that Lanval should be 'pruz e curteis' (113) if he is to attain the supreme joy of her love. Lanval falls instantly in love with her, a *coup de foudre* which is expressed in the same metaphor as that used in *Guigemar*, lines 391-92. The fairy's promise of infinite worldly wealth magically provided has both a literal and metaphorical meaning, in that it suggests the costliness of the fairy's love, while implicitly condemning the hero's inferior treatment at court. The love scene also contains the traditional demand for secrecy, the price of which is the fairy herself. This reflects, of course, the importance of concealing the lady's identity in courtly doctrine, but it is also another aspect of the courtly code which receives some modification in Marie's hands, in that she goes on to present a situation where the breaking of the promise is not wholly to be condemned and the outcome is apparently unimpaired.

The first part of the *lai* ends with Lanval's return to the city on his richly groomed horse. For the first time he is shown to be fearful, with lines 196-200 indicating realistically his state of shock following his encounter with the Other World. This is rapidly succeeded by a description of the new Lanval, who becomes a central figure thanks to his new-found wealth, in contrast to his earlier isolation, an idea which is given full emphasis by the anaphora of lines 209-12 and the further repetition in 214-15. His generosity is directly linked to his frequent intercourse with the fairy, and as a result Lanval is not only fully acccepted by the most courtly of Arthur's knights, but also attracts the attention of the queen.

In the second part of the *lai* Lanval's oath of secrecy is severely tested, and as a consequence of his failure to keep it we see the fairy's threat of withdrawing her love carried out. Yet again Lanval is cast in the role of the outsider, for, despite his general acceptance by his fellow knights, his constant thoughts of his mistress prevent him from participating in the lighthearted activities in the *vergier* (252). The queen's speech to Lanval is a direct and premeditated declaration of love which is lacking in courtly nuance and in *mesure*, while Lanval's reply is not particularly courtly either, reflecting his resentment at being disturbed. The queen's slanderous retort reveals her pique at finding that her excessive trust in her own charms has been misplaced, but her accusation of homosexuality is also an inevitable consequence of Lanval's continuing reputation as a loner so far as women are concerned. In realistic anger she attacks Lanval verbally (283) and hints at getting her own back through her husband. This theme of the temptress rebuffed, which goes back to the Old Testament story of Potiphar's wife, is a familiar one in medieval literature, and is examined more closely by Faverty (*21*). Lanval's reply to the queen constitutes his uncourtly behaviour in the real world which is punished both in an earthly trial and, more importantly, at the level of the supernatural. Justly provoked, he answers angrily and at length, not only revealing the secret of his mistress but indulging in increasing *démesure* by adding insults, although these are not without foundation.

Lines 311-470 present the punishment of Lanval's *démesure* in the initiation of judicial proceedings and in the loss of his fairy mistress. The queen falsely reports to her husband Lanval's description of the fairy (321), and while the king's anger is rightly aroused at this slur on his wife, he seems fairly unconcerned that she should have been propositioned at all. A supernatural element is inherent in the fact that Lanval's loss of his mistress has apparently been instantaneous and he becomes 'pensis . . . e anguissus' (338), terms which Marie formerly applied to undeclared love as well as to lost love. The king's accusation repeats that of the queen, but adds that Lanval's words constitute a slander against his own person (365-67), a charge which Lanval, in his feudal duty, cannot deny, although he knows the truth of his own claim, despite its *folie*. In the long trial scene that follows, where Marie is able to display her knowledge of the legal process, the most significant factor is the command to Lanval to produce his mistress (452), or else suffer dismissal from court, a less severe penalty than that threatened by the king in line 328. This judgement is reported to Lanval, whose plea of his inability to do so is also relayed in indirect speech, a form which hastens the narrative, when the king appears to be under some pressure from his impatient wife.

This haste in matters of temporal justice heralds the sudden and immediate return of the supernatural, which is the major theme in the final part of the *lai*. The arrival of the first pair of maidens has the function of delaying the trial, and the fact that their request takes precedence over it may reflect the courtly attitude towards women which, in literary convention, characterizes Arthur's court. When the trial is resumed the barons are fearful (509), which may be suggestive of some supernatural presence, and then comes the second pair of girls. Lanval denies all knowledge of them, who are, perhaps, meant to be the pair who originally summoned him, since they are differentiated by age, as at line 61. As they are more beautiful than the first couple, Marie gives us more details of them through the eyes of the knights, who are clearly convinced that they surpass the queen in beauty (532), thereby vindicating Lanval's claim. The third and final interruption of the trial is the arrival of the fairy herself and her superiority is indicated at once (550). Her white palfrey also attracts attention and surpasses all others in beauty and costliness (556-58), a sure indication now of the Other World. Slowly and tantalisingly the description moves to its climax as the fairy is announced at court: 'Ceo est la plus bele del mund' (591). Marie has taken more than forty lines to build up to this, and the final comment at last arouses Lanval as he recognizes the fairy and sees at once the significance of her arrival and the importance of her *merci* (599). The description of the fairy continues, and her physical superiority to the queen is stressed as she removes her cloak, which recalls the sensuality of the previous descriptions and silently justifies Lanval's boast.

When the fairy eventually speaks, her declaration is made in the perfect tense, 'j'ai aimé' (615), the same tense as was used in her earlier speech (263-64), which suggests that her love for Lanval does, in fact, continue into the present. Again revealing her supernatural omniscience she goes on to state that the queen is in the wrong and to tell the truth that Lanval, in his loyalty to the king, had concealed. The abrupt departure of the fairy which follows Lanval's acquittal by the court receives little emphasis, but Lanval's decision to follow her is more carefully prepared, as a few lines of seemingly irrelevant detail (533-37) lead up to his dramatic leap onto her horse. Together they ride off to Avalon, the Other World, where the knowledge of their fate is concealed from the mortal story-teller, although it is implied that the outcome is a happy one.

The *lai* of *Lanval*, then, recounts the movements to and from the real and the supernatural, in establishing a love relationship between a fairy and a mortal and in contrasting temporal and other worldly justice. There is a much quoted article by S. Foster Damon (*25*) in which he suggested that the action is solely a product of Lanval's imagination, an enactment of psychological fantasy provoked by the hero's isolation and despondency. If this is to be the case, then Marie de France must have been seven centuries ahead of her time, and it seems more likely that in claiming authenticity for her tales of the supernatural she was appealing to medieval man's acceptance of the Christian and the non-Christian miraculous, rather than attempting the modern rejection of both. Significantly, Christian and pagan elements are shown to be compatible in *Yonec*, where the main theme is that of supernatural transformation, and again the two worlds at times converge.

(b) *Yonec*

The thematic structure of *Yonec* is more complex than that of *Lanval* in that nearly the whole of the latter is subsumed in the

first part of *Yonec*. There, as in *Lanval*, human injustice
prepares the advent of a love affair provided by supernatural
intervention, an affair culminating in tragedy due to human
démesure, during which the mortal lady is able to follow her
dying lover into the realm of the supernatural. In the second part
of *Yonec*, however, the supernatural elements are transformed
into human, Christian ones, where the lovers are reunited in
death and their fate is avenged by their son against a background
of Christian celebration. The story is set in the distant past (11),
as is *Bisclavret*, the third *lai* in which the supernatural has a key
part to play.

The story opens with an inappropriate situation, a young wife
who is married to an aged husband, and whose fate is
comparable to that of the lady in *Milun*. There is no question of
mutual love in this marriage, which takes place solely to provide
an old man with an heir, although he is said to love his wife for
her beauty (24-25). The lady, however, has more than external
qualities (21-22), in contrast to the total absence of courtly
features in her husband. Like the lady in *Guigemar* she is
unnamed, but as before, her role is equal in importance to that
of her lover. It is implied that the harsh treatment she receives
from her husband results in a lack of fertility, which defeats the
purpose of the marriage and threatens the lady's life as she
gradually loses her beauty in her sorrow. The notion of *semblant*
(cf. lines 45-48, 77-80, 215-16, 225-35, 321-22) is crucial to the
action of the *lai*, as is the detail that her husband inspires fear
(42-44), for later it is his cruelty which causes his wife's lover to
be mortally wounded.

The change in the initial unhappy situation is announced in
lines 51-52 by the cliché of the 'début printanier' common in
lyric and epic poetry. In the context of this poem, however, the
reference to birdsong assumes an additional significance, since
Muldumarec will appear in bird form. An indication that
something supernatural might occur is provided by the fact that
the jealous husband goes off hunting, although the motif of the
hunt clearly differs in its function here from that in *Guigemar*.
Once she is left alone the lady's sorrow is renewed by her
awareness of the beginning of spring, traditionally a time for

new love. In her monologue she curses her husband using the
further traditional term 'Cist . . . gelus' (71). She laments the
fact that she is not even allowed to go to church, a detail which
both reinforces the notion of her husband's cruelty and also
introduces a religious note which will become increasingly
important in the course of the *lai*. Her modest demands simply
to be able to converse with other people are not yet suggestive of
infidelity, but her emotion increases as she goes on to curse her
family and her husband, who refuses to die. The monologue
reaches it climax in her longing for a courtly but invisible lover,
and *Lanval* has already illustrated that such occurences were
indeed part of Celtic mythology. She ends with a prayer to God
for such a supernatural event to occur, which contrasts with
Lanval where the hero did not make any specific request for
love.

The lady's prayer is immediately answered in an apparently
non-Christian fashion: a seemingly genuine bird (111-12)
changes into a courtly knight. Like Lanval's fairy he assures the
lady that he has loved her for a long time (cf. the Provençal
amor de lonh, love at a distance), and his feelings are therefore
those of courtly longing rather than of sudden desire. There is
also a suggestion that he is bound by a superior power in that he
could only come when she asked him (131-33). The lady's
request that he should first state his belief in God is a variation
on the theme of a test for the would-be lover, and reveals the
integration of the pagan and the Christian supernatural in
Yonec. Indeed, Muldumarec goes beyond his simple declaration
of faith, which is couched in the conventional religious language
of the time, and offers to receive the sacrament of Holy
Communion, while assuming the guise of the lady herself. Thus,
in her concern to establish her hero as a suitable lover, Marie
shows a complete disregard of the morality of the situation and
uses the sacrament accordingly.

The fatal consequences of *démesure* are spelt out at length
(201-10), and this contrasts again with the speech of Lanval's
fairy, whose warning is less clearly prophetic, since the
consequences of betrayal are less dire. The lady's joy, however,
is such that it causes a total change in her appearance; this is

itself a form of *démesure*, and is soon apparent to the jealous husband. The lady lays herself open to further suspicion by her sudden desire for solitude (239-40), a complete reversal of her earlier feelings, and we are left in no doubt as to the tragic outcome of these events (254-56). The plot to spy on the lovers is an action which Marie describes quite unequivocally as *traïsun*, a crime against love committed by *le felun* (295-96), a comment that reveals her involvement with her characters (see further pp.88-89 below). There is no doubt as to the effectiveness of the trap set for the lover, which is conveyed by the repeated references to the amount of blood shed (312, 316-17). Reproachfully Muldumarec tells his mistress that it is her *semblant* which is killing them both (although the lady's literal death does not occur until much later). Here again we see a requirement of courtly love pursued to the extreme, as in *Chaitivel*, where lack of *mesure* on the part of the lady has fatal consequences, although the type of excess is different in each case. Nonetheless, Muldumarec in his agony comforts his mistress with a further prophecy, this time highly reminiscent of Biblical tradition, that she will bear a son who is to be named Yonec. Here the theme of vengeance through the son is introduced and prepares us for the *lai*'s dénouement, and the certainty of this knowledge consoles the lady.

The departure of the dying lover and the lady's desperate attempt to follow him and join him in death would render this *lai* essentially tragic, were it not for the fact that the main emphasis clearly lies elsewhere, namely in the avenging of the destruction of a courtly love relationship. Thus there follows next the highly improbable (although not explicitly supernatural) escape of Yonec's mistress, not unlike that of Guigemar's lady (*Guigemar*, 673-88). That a pregnant woman can jump twenty feet from her tower without injury to herself or her child is justly described by Marie as miraculous: 'C'est merveille k'el ne s'ocist' (338) and her pursuit of Muldumarec leads her through a landscape clearly evocative of the supernatural. The trail of blood takes her firstly through a hollow hill (346-55), after which she finds herself in a 'mut bel pre' (356) and subsequently in a city of unsurpassed richness

(363-64) which is again close to water (365, 368): evidently she is in the Other World to which her lover belongs. The details again emphasizing its splendour create an effect of suspense leading up to the lady's sorrow as she reaches her dying lover, and the scene between them parallels that already enacted in the real world. Thus we see in the first part of *Yonec* the same intermingling of courtliness and otherworldly mystery that was notable in *Lanval*, before the lady returns to reality and a new life with her husband.

The two parts of the *lai* are linked by a short transitional passage (457-66) in which Yonec grows up to become a truly courtly figure. In the short second part, the predominantly supernatural theme of the first part is transformed into a Christian temporality. This means that the amorality of the beginning is counterbalanced, for, as de Caluwé (*17*, p. 114) has concluded, 'l'importance accordée à l'élément chrétien dans les *Lais* de Marie est directement proportionnelle à l'amoralisme de ses intrigues'. This change is announced by the setting for the final action, the celebration of a holy day, which, since it is the feast of a Celtic saint, is an additional reminder of the worldly Celtic setting. Despite the fact that the husband ought logically to be very old by now, the family set out for the celebrations with the help of a guide. The richness of their own apparel and that of the castle to which they are led serves as a reminder of the supernatural, but the Christian element continues to prevail as they are brought to the abbey within the castle and subsequently attend Mass. The climax is reached with the discovery of a richly decked tomb (498), which affords Marie the opportunity of revealing Muldumarec's actual status, that of a king who died for his beloved. This flashback to the earlier supernatural events is quickly curtailed by the lady's realization of what has happened and she tells her son 'Deus nus ad mené ici' (528), a reminder of that compatibility of Christian and pagan mysteries shown earlier. As soon as Yonec's mother has fulfilled her function of revealing his father's identity she falls dead on the tomb and Yonec is left to fulfil the prophecy of vengeance. Ultimately, then, mother and son receive their due recognition, and a four-line epilogue states that the *lai* is specifically intended to commemorate the suffering inherent in love, an ending which emphasizes the events recounted rather than the characters themselves.

(ii) *The supernatural tests love:* Bisclavret

If it is possible for the supernatural to intervene in human affairs to remedy injustice by the provision of love, it is equally possible that some supernatural factor may constitute a test of human love. This seems to me to be the main theme of *Bisclavret*, where the revelation that the husband is a werewolf and therefore only partly human puts the wife's love to a severe test—one which she not only fails but attempts to avert by means of treachery aimed at destroying her husband's human aspect. As we have already seen in *Equitan*, such behaviour must be punished, according to Marie's ethics, because the husband is not an unworthy character. The penalty need not be death, and *Bisclavret* contains the supreme example of a punishment devised to fit the crime. In this *lai* the supernatural first tests well-established marital love (15-134) and then avenges the treachery (135-314).

The poem begins with a choice of title which, as we shall see also in *Laüstic*, is a linguistic choice, as opposed to the thematic alternatives offered in *Eliduc* and *Chaitivel*. *Bisclavret*'s prologue has a primarily explanatory function, not just with respect to the title, but also in defining the nature of a werewolf. We shall, however, see in the course of the story that the courtly nature of the man overcomes the normally ferocious aspect of the beast. (For a further discussion of Marie's treatment of the familiar werewolf theme see Bambeck (2).) More than elsewhere, the prologue emphasizes the importance of past time, due to the obviously legendary nature of the werewolf itself, although Marie is careful to point out that she herself has been told about the hero of the story (16).

The knight whose dual nature is the subject of the poem is not only courtly (17-18) but is also loved by his lord and fellow knights, and this is a feature which assumes considerable importance in the course of the story. Unlike the women in *Chaitivel* and *Equitan*, his wife is not wholly lacking in courtliness, since the married couple are clearly shown to be compatible (23). The flaw in this happy relationship is Bisclavret's habitual disappearance for three days each week, when no-one knows where he is. In the light of our knowledge of his true nature it is not surprising that he returns home 'joius e liez' (30), but to his wife this is obviously a source of worry, since it might well be supposed that he has another love interest elsewhere. The truth is revealed in some dramatic exchanges between husband and wife (32-96), where elements of courtliness and the supernatural are again related. The lady plays on her husband's emotions by exaggerating her fear of losing him, which would, in true courtly fashion, precipitate her own death. Her husband's reply warns her immediately of the evil which will befall them if he answers her questions, accurately foreseeing (as did Muldumarec in *Yonec*) the precise consequences of his revelation. His wife, however, persists until he tells her, and the man's reply contrasts in its complete openness with his wife's cunning and suspicious nature. Showing no apparent shock the lady continues to nag him, with the key question 's'il se despuille u vet vestu' (69), which perhaps indicates her familiarity with the nature of such beasts and, already, her evil intent. When Bisclavret reluctantly reveals where his clothes are hidden, a specifically Christian element is introduced into the *lai*. The clothes are near a chapel where the knight has received 'grant bien' (92), and this again indicates a certain compatibility between the Christian and pagan supernatural, such as that already noted in *Yonec*.

Bisclavret's wife is treated throughout with a certain amount of psychological insight. In lines 97-99 she reveals for the first time her emotion at what she hears. Suffering perhaps from delayed shock, her initial understandable reaction is to withdraw from intimacy with her husband (102). It is also not surprising that the effect of her husband's revelation is for her to run to an admirer of long standing and express a desire to become his mistress. However, the lady needs more than a lover; her ulterior motive is to get someone to commit her act of betrayal for her, although the crime is clearly seen by Marie to be hers (126), and this will be borne out by the eventual punishment which the pair receive. The remainder of the action revolves around the character of the king. Once again the motif of a hunt is used to herald the occurrence of something unusual, and the normal processes of nature are reversed, as the wolf turns towards his pursuers and, in the first of a series of human rather than animal actions, appears to beg the king for mercy (147-48). The king's justifiable fear may also be interpreted in terms of fear in the presence of the supernatural, as he recognizes 'entente e sen' (157) in the wolf.

Henceforth the stress is laid on the human characteristics inherent in the beast rather than on those of the wolf in the man, as Marie engages the reader's sympathy for her hero. He is eventually credited with human courtly qualities (179), and is remarkable for the love he displays for his king. Yet, in attacking his wife's new husband, Bisclavret continues to possess the omniscience of a supernatural creature and can only be restrained by the king himself. This behaviour is at once acknowledged to be out of character and is described in human terms as being 'sanz reisun' (208). The second deviation from normal behaviour occurs when Bisclavret is brought into the presence of his wife, whose concern for her appearance is suggested in line 228, 'Avenantement se appareilot', a detail which is rapidly to assume considerable significance. The severity of Bisclavret's attack in biting off his wife's nose, and its suitability as a punishment for a vain woman, receives explicit comment (236), but the wolf receives no sympathy from the court until 'un sages hum' intervenes and points out the significance of the two events.

With a final stroke of realism Marie tells us how the wolf is unwilling or unable to be transformed when his clothes are restored (280), and again it falls to the wise man to point out Bisclavret's human modesty and need for privacy. Then, as in *Lanval*, the guilty couple have to suffer earthly justice as well as supernatural revenge, and are condemned to exile for having betrayed Bisclavret. Retribution continues to be inflicted on the female offspring of the bigamous union, who are born *esnasees* (314) and the humour of this final detail is stressed by the pun of line 313, 'senz nes sunt nees'. Thus, she concludes, Marie has composed a *lai* of true adventure, although its import lies less in its claim to veracity than in the morality which it upholds. The supernatural in *Bisclavret*, in fact, puts two types of loyalty to the test. That of marital fidelity is failed by the wife, who is duly punished, but feudal loyalty, in terms of the relationship between king and vassal, is upheld, although, as in *Lanval*, the eventual fate of the hero is unknown.

6 *Aspects of Fatal Love*: Les deus amanz, Laüstic, Chevrefoil

The three *lais* which remain to be discussed all share a predominantly tragic atmosphere. In the case of *Les deus amanz* this is established in the course of the *lai*, while in the other two it is present throughout. In the first two *lais* the tragedy is precipitated by *démesure* on the part of one of the lovers, the lack of discretion of the youth in *Les deus amanz* being complemented by that of the lady in *Laüstic*, and this results in the death of both lovers in the former and the symbolic death of mutual love in the latter. These *lais* stand in contrast to *Chaitivel*, where the lady did not share the tragic fate of her suitors and, to a lesser extent, to *Equitan* where, despite the fatal outcome, it seems to me that there are no truly tragic overtones in the poem. On the other hand it is inescapable that *Chaitivel*, *Equitan* and *Yonec* are all *lais* in which some form of *démesure* does precipitate tragedy; the fact that any thematic categories devised and imposed upon the *lais* by critics necessarily overlap to a certain extent is perhaps indicative of the thematic unity of the whole of Marie's collecion. *Chevrefoil*, however, does stand a little apart from the other poems in that it describes just one episode within the framework of a well-known love story, but the overwhelmingly tragic atmosphere which derives from the familiar ending of the story of Tristan and Iseut clearly relates it to the other two *lais* under discussion in this chapter.

(i) *Les deus amanz*

The prologues to *Les deus amanz* and *Chevrefoil* both contain an element not to be found in any of the other *lais*, namely a specific indication of the death of the lovers. In the former it is clear that the *lai* will tell the *aventure* of their death (2-4), while in the latter it is suggested that death, although inevitable, is not the subject of the *lai*, which is rather the story of their 'amur que tant fu fine' (*Chevrefoil*, 8). The definition of *Les deus amanz* as the story of children in love (3) contains both a hint of pathos and, perhaps, a suggestion as to the innocent behaviour of the protagonists. The poem is unusual in that it is associated with a particular place (and, moreover, a place in Normandy rather than Brittany) and is the only example in Marie's collection of a specifically local legend. However, the main part of the *lai* has a pattern similar to those already examined in chapter 4 which centre around obstacles to love. Here we are presented with a problem (the lover's Herculean task in winning his princess), a solution is offered (a magic potion) and this is rejected in an act of childish pride and folly which precipitates the death of both characters.

The fact that *démesure* is an essential ingredient of this poem is clear from the outset, in that it takes two forms, the first being the king's over-possessive attitude towards his daughter. As in *Le Fresne* the action of the *lai* is initiated by gossip, which is a slanderous rumour about the nature of the relationship between father and daughter, and *démesure* is inevitably present in the king's decision to ask the impossible of the girl's suitors to avoid losing her. Lines 49 to 142 present a double obstacle corresponding to the two-fold *démesure* in the poem. Firstly the father's plan is thwarted by his daughter's falling in love, and secondly the young man of her choice is confronted by the task of climbing the hill. The young man is introduced as courtly (50), but already there is a flaw in his character, his excessive ambition, which places him alongside two of Marie's other heroes, Guigemar and Equitan, all three exemplifying a different kind of fault. The secrecy which surrounds the young people's love necessarily entails suffering, particularly since the relationship is a legitimate one, and this is something that the youth is perhaps too immature to endure beyond his initial patience (69-70), hence his suggestion of an elopement. Both he and the princess seem to be sufficiently realistic to acknowledge his inability to fulfil the allotted task, at least by natural means. In the girl's alternative solution of a strengthening herbal potion there is no question of supernatural intervention, simply a belief in the 'art de phisike' practised by a woman of good birth and reputation. Thus when the young man arrives in Salerno he undergoes some body-building treatment before being given the vital potion.

With the return to the main action at the beginning of the final section (143-240) the king grants permission for the youth to try for his daughter's hand, confident that he will fail (149-51). Marie adds some practical and realistic detail in the girl's decision to diet and to wear the minimum of clothing to make her lover's task easier. Nonetheless, the young man's tendency to *démesure* begins to manifest itself again in the form of excessive enthusiasm. As the crowds assemble he is the first to arrive (168) and the tragic outcome, due to his rejecting the magic potion, is made quite clear by Marie (178-79), who relates it specifically to the lack of *mesure*. *Démesure* is associated with the *joie* which the youth has found in love (182) and echoes the indiscretion described in *Lanval*, while presenting another, more human, illustration of the connection between the two ideas made by the Provençal poets. In the course of his ordeal the youth reveals his misguided belief in his own capacities, in his reluctance to stop long enough even to drink the potion. The girl's growing anxiety is reflected in the boy's increasing obstinacy, a scene which culminates in his sudden and dramatic death (205). Pathetically, the girl attempts to revive him with the drink, only to throw it away in her despair and frustration. The detail of lines 218-19 shows that it did indeed have life-giving properties and that it would have worked, had human weakness not rejected it. There is a strong echo of the death of Tristan and Iseut as recounted in Thomas's *Roman de Tristan*, as the unfortunate princess dies of a broken heart. The lovers are buried together, and a brief epilogue, very similar to that in *Bisclavret*, tells of the purpose of the *lai*, to keep alive the legend and therefore its moral.

(ii) *Laüstic*

In *Les deus amanz* we have been considering a *lai* where the action was reduced to a fairly routine notion of a physical test and where a tragic atmosphere resulting from youthful *démesure* predominates, despite occasional lighter touches. In *Laüstic* and *Chevrefoil* the tragic note is complemented by a particularly realistic treatment of emotions which is perhaps all the more apparent because of the lack of action in the short poems themselves. The intensity of feelings expressed in the limited framework of these two *lais* probably explains why they have become the best known of Marie's poems. The name *Laüstic* represents a symbol of tragic love as described in the poem, and for this reason the title receives emphasis from its French and English alternatives. The *lai* itself has three main elements, namely the description of a platonic love affair (7-56), another example of double *démesure* (57-120), and the outcome of this and the symbolizing of lost love in the form of spilt blood and a dead bird (121-56).

The presentation of characters at the beginning again exemplifies Marie's technique of description by omission. We are given details of two of the three, firstly the courtly wife of one of the two unnamed knights and secondly the young man who is the couple's neighbour. The longer description accorded to the latter establishes him as a worthy hero and a courtly lover (17-22) and there are sound psychological reasons why his love is reciprocated: his fame (27) and his proximity (29). The love affair is necessarily secret and platonic, and the lovers' discretion is approvingly stressed by Marie. Nonetheless it is clearly suggested that they would have preferred a more intimate relationship to their simple communication over the wall and the exchange of gifts, which is as close as they ever come to physical contact. Ironically, the lovers' proximity actually underlines their separation, because of the single dividing wall between the two houses, and the high wall and the bedroom window have obvious symbolic and sexual overtones.

With the arrival of spring, the clichés of flowers and birds receive additional significance (as in *Yonec*), for it is a bird, generally the symbol of love and happiness, which is to be transformed into a symbol of frustration and tragedy. Lines 63-68 give an indication of sexual desire on the part of both knight and lady, and we are then introduced to the first form of *démesure*. As in *Les deus amanz* the initial fault is less dramatic than the second, but it is nonetheless the cause of the greater *démesure* and therefore of the final tragedy. The lady's indiscretion lies in her continual rising at night to see her lover from her window (71, 79-80). Her reply to her husband's understandably persistent inquiries as to what she is doing centres on the nightingale. Given that the bird is a well-established symbol of love, and that her speech is both exaggerated and ambiguous (see especially lines 87-90), it is scarcely surprising that her husband, already irritated at having his sleep disturbed, should become both angry and suspicious. This anger rapidly turns into an obsession, which becomes the second and more destructive form of *démesure*, and this is first manifested in the elaborate and ridiculous lengths to which he goes to ensnare the bird. When he is at last successful, a certain ambiguity appears in the husband's words as he tells his wife that henceforth she may rest in peace, 'gisir en peis', the well-known formula perhaps anticipating the death of her love.

The lady's emotions on hearing this are, again quite realistically, sorrow and anger at the loss of her excuse for seeing her lover. The bird's death is occasioned by her request that her husband should give it to her — it is reasonable to suppose that she intends releasing it — and, no doubt, by his anger at the strength of her feeling. Thus the second form of *démesure* lies in the husband's extreme reaction in strangling the bird and throwing its corpse at his wife, leaving a bloodstain on her heart, and storming out of the room. This action constitutes a physical assault on his wife, which is perhaps unique in courtly poetry, and the blood of the bird is a clear symbol of her broken heart and lost love. It does not, I think, symbolize the death of physical love (*pace* Cottrell, *14*, p. 503), since Marie does not tell us of any such relationship. In addition, the husband is now characterized as *vileins* (116), being overtly in opposition to courtly behaviour.

The final strand of the *lai* begins with the pathos of the scene where the lady weeps over the dead bird, 'le cors petit' (121), a description which, sadly, might be applied to the lovers' relationship as well. Not wishing her lover to think that she has lost interest in him, the lady devises a means of communication similar to that used by Tristan in *Chevrefoil*, namely to make an object (here the lavishly wrapped bird) into both a message and symbol of love. The richness of the material in which the bird is placed indicates the strength of that love and anticipates a similar treatment of it by the lover. The knight's reaction is one not of anger but of sorrow, and this is reminiscent of the behaviour of Muldumarec in *Yonec* when he is himself ensnared by a jealous husband. The dead bird becomes totally a symbol of eternal love as it is placed in a casket of precious stones, which is, in effect, a reliquary. At the end of the *lai* a final reminder of its title recalls the symbolic importance of the name of the nightingale.

(iii) *Chevrefoil*

The *lai* of *Chevrefoil* has attracted perhaps more attention than any other of Marie's poems because it recounts an episode in the story of Tristan and Iseut which is not known from any other source. Adams and Hemming (*1*, p. 212), among others, have suggested that its importance lies in its preserving traces of the primitive version of the Tristan legend, which underlies the better known works of Eilhart, Béroul and Thomas. Clearly Marie was fully familiar with the legend in both its oral and written versions (4-5) and expects her readers to be acquainted with it as well, since knowledge of the characters and their background is taken for granted. As Adams and Hemming have pointed out (*1*, p. 206), the *lai* is concerned with Tristan's period in exile and ends with the suggestion that eventual reconciliation with his uncle, Mark, might be possible (106), although in all other versions he can return to the court only in disguise.

However, we are here concerned with *Chevrefoil* in the context of a collection of *lais*, and apart from its obvious wider associations, it shares many of the outstanding features of the other eleven. Perhaps even more than *Les deus amanz* and *Laüstic*, *Chevrefoil* is representative of Marie's conception of tragic love. There is no hint of *démesure* or any other uncourtly behaviour on the part of either of the lovers: they are the ultimate embodiment of courtly love, and stand out from others by reason of their 'amur que tant fu fine' (8), and their tragic end, due entirely to this love, is well-known from the outset (9-10). Marie also forewarned us of inevitable death in *Equitan* (184) and *Les deus amanz* (4), but in both these cases *démesure* was to blame. Perhaps then, the message that Marie intended us to draw from *Chevrefoil* is that courtly love as traditionally presented is inherently tragic, doomed to failure. Certainly the other *lais* we have examined seem to bear this out. Unhappiness, even death, results from human imperfections, unless some supernatural element intervenes. Although Marie condones extra-marital relationships where the lovers are compatible and worthy of each other, the Tristan legend shows that even so, tragedy cannot necessarily be averted.

At the beginning of the *lai* (11-28) we are given a short indication of its place in the Tristan legend. Lines 19-20 allude to the period of exile described in the two so-called *Folies* (*23* and *24*), where Tristan is driven mad in his grief at being parted from his mistress, and Marie adds a comment of her own on her favourite topic of loyalty in love: separation inevitably causes sorrow (22-24), as we have seen in the 'courtly' *lais* of *Eliduc* and *Guigemar*. In Tristan's case such a separation is unbearable and he returns to live a secret life in the forest to be near the queen. It is interesting that Marie is following closely the technique used on a broader scale by Thomas throughout his *Roman de Tristan*, where a broad generalization on the nature of love is followed by its application to one particular situation.

With news of the queen's expected arrival (43) the picture of the general amusement at court (42) is echoed in the individual happiness, albeit fleeting, of the lover. There then follows a passage which has generated a considerable amount of critical writing and divergence of opinion. Marie's text tells us first that on the crucial day of the queen's journey Tristan cut himself a 'bastun' of hazel and wrote his name on it: 'De sun cutel escrit sun nun' (54). He is confident that the queen will see it and recognize her lover's presence. While some critics have questioned how this might be possible (a survey of opinions is presented by Hatcher, *30*), since Iseut would obviously be on horseback, this does seem to be underestimating Tristan's resourcefulness and need not detain us here, particularly since Marie seems to be suggesting that a precedent has already been set for this means of communication anyway (57-58). The major interpretative problem lies not in Iseut's realizing the significance of the stick, but rather in what was written on it. Marie tells us quite unambiguously:

> Ceo fu la summe de l'escrit
> Qu'il li aveit mandé e dit (61-62)

which is followed by fourteen lines apparently of message, and two of direct address.

The most likely explanation is that Iseut, on seeing the name of Tristan, will read into it the content of the 'message' of lines 63-76, and that the remaining couplet is Tristan himself speaking aloud in his emotion at the interpretation he envisages. Some critics, however, have suggested that this message is to be taken as literally written down, either on the stick or in a previous communication. Another idea, put forward by Cagnon (*10*), is that Tristan was using a system of character writing (the so-called Ogamic tradition) where comparatively few symbols convey a wealth of meaning. However, whichever interpretation is preferred, Marie's interest clearly lies in what is said rather than how it is said, and Tristan's message is a simple one: he cannot live without his mistress. This is reinforced by a romantic, although botanically inaccurate, image of the mutual dependence of the hazel and the honeysuckle, which can only survive when intertwined. I believe that it is also significant that Marie should have taken the honeysuckle for her title, since it reflects the beauty of the relationship as well as the sorrow, and that this is not outweighed by the importance of the stick which most critics see as the symbolic object at the centre of the *lai*.

In the last section of the *lai* (79-106) the message is seen and understood and a brief but joyful meeting ensues. There is a certain pathos in the fact that such a fleeting encounter nonetheless produces such *joie* that Tristan is inspired to compose a *lai* on the strength of it. The main subject of it, as we have shown, is the commemoration of Tristan's message and the queen's interpretation of it.

In conclusion, then, Marie presents us with three *lais* which each convey slightly different aspects of tragic love. In *Les deus amanz* the protagonists die together, owing to *démesure* on the part of the youth, while in *Laüstic* the same failing on the part of the lady implies a fatal end to love itself, the lovers being united in a single symbol of tragedy. Much the same may be said of *Chevrefoil*, for although there is no element of indiscretion here, the reunion of the lovers cannot prevent their inevitable death, and again love and death are inextricably interwoven in a single symbol, that of the honeysuckle and the hazel.

7 Marie's Contribution to Twelfth-Century Literature

The individuality of Marie de France which justifies the continuing study of her poems and their place in the history of early French literature lies in two particular features of her writing: the ethical code which governs the behaviour of her characters and her stylistic technique. We have seen in the preceding chapters many examples of Marie's ability to take well-known literary motifs and use them for her own purposes, thereby adding a wealth of literary allusion to the stories she has to tell. That this procedure does not result in a highly disparate and fragmented set of poetic compositions is mainly due to these two elements; her moral attitude gives thematic unity to the collection of poems, while her style unites them linguistically, and it seems appropriate to devote this concluding chapter to a brief appraisal of each.

(i) *Marie's ethics*

The protagonists in Marie's poems are nearly all shown to need love, whether they have already found it in an established relationship or are in search of it. As Ménard points out (*36*, p. 137), love is seen as the supreme good for the individual, and it is thus placed above society's demands of chivalry and, often, of marriage, which, after all, would seldom have been a love match. Marie therefore portrays characters seeking supreme joy in a relationship which is platonic only when circumstances prevent it from being otherwise, as in *Laüstic*, and marriage appears as no more than the logical consequence of such a relationship rather than as an end in itself. However, although such a view is naturally contrary to the teaching of the Church, Marie's characters are far from being amoral. On the contrary, this disregard of marriage, and indeed of adultery, is possible only because of the carefully formulated moral code to which

Marie's lovers adhere. Writing of *Le Fresne*, the only *lai* in which the couple are actually said to live happily ever after in marriage, Foulon (*26*, p. 212) sees 'une sorte de conclusion morale très originale, réunissant l'amour courtois, l'union libre et la conception chrétienne du mariage', but it must be emphasized that this third element is not normally present.

At the heart of Marie's ethics is the concept of loyalty, without which any personal relationship is doomed to failure. In the *Lais* two forms of fidelity are of paramount importance. Firstly, the successful relationship between lord and vassal depends on feudal loyalty, and it is this which rescues Bisclavret from his fate as a werewolf when he has lost the loyalty of his wife. In other *lais* feudal loyalty is often presented as a quality in the courtly knight, although the main interest may be focussed instead on his fidelity in love. Thus mutual loyalty between king and vassal is mentioned at the beginning of *Eliduc*:

> Elidus aveit un seignur,
> Reis de Brutaine la meinur,
> Que mut l'amot e cherisseit,
> E il lëaument le serveit. (29-32)

while Lanval is characterized by his fidelity to the king whom he has served for a long time for no reward, hence his refusal to accept and subsequently to reveal the queen's advances, as he says to her:

> Lungement ai servi le rei;
> Ne li voil pas mentir ma fei.' (271-72)

Secondly, the same mutual fidelity is a prerequisite of a successful relationship between man and woman both within and outside marriage, and this often makes considerable demands on the patience of the lovers. Thus Milun and his mistress are ultimately reunited thanks to their unquestioning acceptance of their fate for twenty years, until their son is old enough to take the necessary action. The same quality is shown by the lovers in *Laüstic*, who maintain an unpromising liaison for an unspecified length of time, 'Lungement se sunt entr'amé' (57), before even this is brought abruptly to an end. Unselfish love is characterized above all by loyalty, as Eliduc recognizes when he laments his seemingly dead mistress:

Bele, ja fuissiez vus reïne,
Ne fust l'amur leale e fine
Dunt vus m'amastes lëaument (943-45)

and since he too has pledged his loyalty to her (690-96) they find
in their eventual marriage the ideal 'parfit'amur' (1150).

The absence of loyalty, whether in feudal or amorous
relationships, which includes the marriage of compatible
partners, is inevitably destructive. It is significant that Marie
several times uses the breakdown of feudal obligations to set her
action in motion: Eliduc is forced to leave court because of
jealousy, while Lanval is isolated within it. More seriously, for
these are temporary states of affairs, Equitan's disregard for his
duty to his senechal in seducing his wife leads inexorably to his
punishment, as well as to the death of the woman who has been
equally disloyal to her husband.

Fidelity is thus always rewarded in some way in Marie's
poems, even though this may be no more than earthly
vengeance, as in *Yonec*, where the couple can be united only in
death. Conversely, lack of such a quality is necessarily punished
to a greater or lesser extent, and this brings us to Marie's idea of
justice in the *Lais*. We have seen already how punishments are
devised to fit the crime in *Bisclavret*, although more normally
shortcomings in the characters are punished either by the
temporary loss of love or by death, depending on the gravity of
the offence. In *Bisclavret* it seems that the demands made on the
werewolf's wife are seen as barely tolerable, and her failure and
subsequent treachery are punished not by death but by
disfigurement, although it must be remembered that since
Bisclavret is saved from his fate, death may not in any case be a
suitable punishment for his wife. Several times Marie
demonstrates that wrongful action rebounds on its instigator. In
Le Fresne it is the mother's slander of her neighbour which
threatens her downfall, as she herself acknowledges: 'jeo
meïsmes me jugai' (79) and 'sur mei en est turné le pis' (86),
while *Equitan* provides a more serious example, which leads to
Marie's concluding comment:

Tel purcace le mal d'autrui
Dunt le mals [tut] revert sur lui. (309-10)

If the originally feudal concept of loyalty is at the heart of the relationships described by Marie, and the lack of it is to be punished, so too is the medieval idea of *mesure*, and we have already seen how *démesure* in its different forms is also punished in a variety of ways. *Démesure* is taken to the extreme in *Chaitivel* in the form of the lady's inability to choose a suitor and also in the young knights' excessive zeal in her service, and this is punished by death and disability, just as the lack of self-control is the immediate cause of the death of the more culpable lovers in *Equitan*, and the outcome is equally tragic in *Yonec*, *Les deus amanz* and, symbolically, *Laüstic*. In *Lanval*, however, we see Marie more sympathetic to the *démesure* of her hero, and the loss of his fairy mistress is a temporary punishment inflicted by a supernatural being who is ready to save her lover from additional punishment at the hands of earthly justice.

Finally, Marie's ethics do not make demands only on the behaviour of her lovers, but on their very nature, that is to say they must be a compatible pair. For Marie this means compatibility in terms of courtly characteristics, which include notably an absence of jealousy and similarity in age, as well as social factors. Thus the social distance between the lovers in *Equitan* leads to tragedy, and it also is significant that in this *lai* the king is aware that such an adulterous relationship is wrong, although he persists in it:

'E si jo l'aim, jeo ferai mal' (71)

However, where the lovers are thought to be compatible adultery is not a stumbling block. In *Yonec* and *Laüstic* the conduct of the husband excuses the wife's actual or desired adultery, while in *Eliduc* and, arguably, in *Chevrefoil*, the courtly qualities of the couple themselves ensure the continuation of the liaison. Similarly a pre-marital relationship is condoned in *Milun* and *Le Fresne* because of the couple's suitability, which Marie makes clear both by endowing each partner with all the qualities she considers essential (often summed up in the simple term *curteis*) and by celebrating their mutual love. We have of course seen already how the absence of courtly epithets in the description of one of a couple suggests that they are unsuited to each other, e.g. *Equitan*, 31-37 and

Bisclavret, 21-22. It might also be noted that Marie several times
shows herself to be conscious of unnatural forms of love. We
have seen references to suspected homosexuality in both
Guigemar and *Lanval* and there is an implicit accusation of
incest in *Les deus amanz*. As a result her conception of ideal love
comes across even more forcefully.

The notion of compatibility is taken to the extreme in
Guigemar, where very precise demands are made on the hero
and his as yet unknown lady, if he is to be healed of his wounds.
In the same *lai* we see this desirable courtly relationship offset by
uncourtly lust, evidenced in the behaviour of Meriadus who
hopes to win the lady by force, and this in turn is punished by
the loss of the lady and of his own life. As the *lai* of *Guigemar*
indicates, Marie imposes her own moral code on all her
characters, not just the chief protagonists, and the behaviour of
the minor characters thus forms an essential part of the action
and adds to the thematic unity of the collection of poems.

(ii) *Marie's style*

Perhaps because Marie's writing lacks the sophistication of a
writer such as Chrétien de Troyes, critical opinion has not
generally seen her style in a very favourable light. Ménard
quotes Bédier's dismissive comment that Marie shows 'aucune
splendeur dans le style' and himself points to her lack of imagery
and small range of vocabulary, which result in 'une certaine
grisaille stylistique' (*36*, p. 205). A study by Biller (*4*) of
rhetorical figures found in early medieval French poetry has
shown that although poor in rhetorical tropes as well as in the
so-called 'figures de pensée' (comparison, allegory, parenthesis
etc.), Marie's writing draws quite extensively on figures
involving repetition, usually for emphatic effect. Linguistic
parallelism has also been noted by Frey (*27*) to reinforce the
couplings of themes and persons which he has studied in the
poems. Beyond this, however, Marie's style has commanded
little attention, the most common view being that it is
characterized by a certain restraint and limpidity and little else.
Indeed Marie on occasions shows rather a disregard for

rhetorical conventions, as for instance in her portraits (e.g. of the fairy in *Lanval*) where the lady's features are listed in an order which is not quite the 'correct' one. However, the fact that Marie does not aspire to elaborate rhetorical heights does not preclude us from examining the features of her style which convey the impression of a simple eloquence and which confer a linguistic unity on her collection of *Lais*.

The essence of Marie's style seems to me to lie in her ability to combine two opposite linguistic tendencies. Firstly, she frequently displays a marked preference for economy of expression. For example, a fast-moving narrative is often achieved through the listing of successive actions, as shown in this couplet in *Guigemar*, where the time element is completely removed:

> Repose s'est, sa plaie dolt,
> Puis est levez, aler s'en volt (189-90)

Similarly we have seen how the action may be hastened through the interplay of direct and indirect speech forms. Significantly, it is often the most important parts of a conversation which are rapidly conveyed, and therefore stressed, in indirect speech. In *Equitan*, for instance, the lady's elaborate plans for removing her husband, which are recounted in twenty lines of direct speech (241-60), are followed by a mere two lines in which Equitan's agreement is stated and the action speeds up again:

> Li reis li ad tut graanté
> Qu'il en ferat sa volonté (261-62)

This technique is used particularly in scenes in which lovers declare their feelings. In *Le Fresne* Gurun makes his declaration of love in twelve lines of direct speech (277-91), and this is counterbalanced by Fresne's rapid acceptance of him:

> Cele que durement l'amot
> Bien otriat ceo que li plot (289-90)

This juxtaposition of passages of direct and indirect speech also has the function of creating some stylistic variety in the narrative which is otherwise difficult to achieve within the restricted framework of the *lai*, and many examples of this may be found, as, for instance, in *Les deus amanz* lines 76-120, where seven lines of reported speech are followed by 32 lines of direct speech and the episode is concluded with four lines of narrative; similarly in *Yonec* the knight's declaration of love is followed by the lady's brief acceptance of him in indirect speech (138-40) and a few lines of narrative, before he continues with his profession of faith.

Linguistic economy is also achieved in Marie's description of her characters, especially through her use of adjectives, to the extent that, as we have seen, their absence is in itself highly significant. The fact that she uses the familiar courtly epithets such as *sage, pruz, vaillanz, curteis* and so on is not to be seen as a lack of originality, for the evocative power of these terms is such that a whole code of conduct is conjured up by them. Equally, Marie uses the terms of suffering ambiguously, as in *Guigemar*, so that two fields of meaning, physical pain and love, may be evoked by them. Related to this, as a means of achieving economical expression, is the writer's use of allusion through the inclusion of readily recognizable motifs which again avert the need for elaborate description. Thus the passage from the real world to the realm of the supernatural is conveyed in *Yonec* by the inclusion of a hollow hill, on the other side of which everything is beautiful:

> . . . fors de la hoge [est] issue
> E en un mut bel pre venue (355-56)

No further indication of the Other World is called for following this familiar motif, particularly since we are already well aware of Muldumarec's supernatural character. On the other hand, where Marie does wish to emphasize a supernatural feature she uses longer descriptions which are marked above all by the use of superlatives. In *Lanval* the motif of running water as indicating the supernatural is reinforced by the long description of the maidens from the Other World of whom Marie says 'Unc n'en ot veü[es] plus beles' (56) and the superlatives proliferate when she comes to describe the fairy herself. Even so, this may also be regarded as a form of economical description, in that the superlatives function as indicators of supernatural qualities and further elaboration is unnecessary.

By contrast, the second ingredient of Marie's style is the extensive use of forms of repetition, which generally have a purely stylistic effect, that of emphasis, as opposed to the thematic function fulfilled by her more economical forms of expression. A very characteristic device is the use of pairs of nearly synonymous terms linked together for emphasis. Thus at the beginning of *Guigemar* we find synonymic pairs relating to a variety of concepts, such as time:

> Quant fu venu *termes e tens*
> Kë il aveit *eage e sens* (45-46)

or events:

> La ont tuz jurz *estrif e guerre* (53)

or possibly character:

> Li vadlet fu *sages e pruz* (43)

and in the same *lai* there is an accumulation of such terms to describe the hero feeling the pangs of love for the first time (392, 394, 398, 401, 404, 412). In *Le Fresne* pairs of words are used to convey both Gurun's love for Fresne and the widespread esteem in which she is held:

> Li chevaler ki l'amena
> Mut la cheri e mut l'ama
> E tut si humme e si servant
> N'i out un sul, petit ne grant,
> Pur sa franchise ne l'amast
> E ne cherist e honurast. (307-12)

This extract also exemplifies another very familiar feature of Marie's style, the use of negatives to express universality, found, too, for example, in *Milun* (301), *Guigemar* (53-56) and *Yonec* (460). Synonyms are also used towards the end of *Bisclavret* to express the affection between king and vassal:

> Li reis le curut enbracier,
> Plus de cent feiz l'acole e baise. (300-1)

Marie also uses literal repetition to stress the point she is making. Perhaps the most obvious example is the anaphora in *Lanval*, where the repetition of the hero's name stresses his rehabilitation at Arthur's court:

> Lanval donout les riches duns,
> Lanval aquitout les prisuns,
> Lanval vesteit les jugleürs,
> Lanval feseit les granz honurs:

> N'i ot estrange ne privé
> A ki Lanval n'eüst doné.
> Mut ot Lanval joie e deduit:
> U seit par jur u seit par nuit,
> S'amie peot veer sovent,
> Tut est a sun comandement. (209-18)

However, this is more than just a borrowing from the textbook of rhetoric. The structure of lines 209-12 may also be seen as reflecting the gossip about Lanval, with each line conveying what is being said about him. The continued repetition of the hero's name in lines 214-15 has the effect of linking his new reputation at court to its cause, his association with his fairy mistress. This then receives its own emphasis in the use of a synonymic pair *joie e deduit* and in the antonyms of line 216.

The important concepts of Marie's poetry may also receive stress from their repetition, which this time involves the reiteration of whole lines rather than single words. Thus her idea of just retribution is emphasized by its repetition in *Equitan*:

> Sur lui est le mal revertiz (299)

and

> Dunt le mals [tut] revert sur lui (310)

and there is a near repetition of the same idea in *Le Fresne*:

> 'Kar jeo meïsmes me jugai' (79)
> 'Vers mei meïsmes [mes]errai' (470)

The repetition of the same parts of speech both with and without similar meaning is a further source of emphasis as, for example, in the description of Guigemar's plight after receiving his wound in the thigh, where adverbs are repeated:

> Mult anguissusement se pleint.
> De sa chemise estreitement
> Sa plaie bende fermement. (138-40)

The repetition of adverbs of quantity has already been noted, and an example of the familiar repetition of *mut* in conjunction with an enumeration of place names, again for emphasis, is found at the beginning of *Milun* to convey the hero's formidable reputation:

> Mut par esteit bons chevaliers
> Francs [e] hardiz, curteis e fiers,

> Mut fu coneüz en Irlande,
> En Norweïë e en Guhtlande;
> En Loengrë e en Albanie
> Eurent plusurs de lui envie:
> Pur sa prüesce iert mut amez
> E de muz princes honurez. (13-20)

Apart from these two constant features of Marie's style, economy and repetition, other characteristics occur at different points in the collection of poems. For example, Marie's realism has been commented on a number of times in the course of this book and this must be counted an important factor in her composition, as must her touches of humour. The author's inclination to laugh at some of her characters finds its expression in a number of ways. In *Laüstic* it is exaggeration, in the elaborate lengths the husband goes to in his efforts to catch a tiny bird, and this is expressed linguistically in Marie's familiar negatives and also in a pair of synonyms:

> Il n'ot vallet en sa meisun
> Ne face engin, reis u laçun
> Puis les mettent par le vergier;
> N'i ot codre ne chastainier
> U il ne mettent laz u glu,
> Tant que pris l'unt e retenu. (95-100)

In *Guigemar* the forthright description of the eunuch priest raises a smile, again at the expense of a jealous husband:

> Uns vielz prestres blancs e floriz
> Guardout la clef de cel postiz;
> Les plus bas membres out perduz:
> Autrement ne fust pas creüz (255-58)

and the husband is once again the object of the desperate lament of the lady in *Yonec*, which is nonetheless tinged with humour:

> Il ne purrat jamés murir.
> Quant il dut estre baptiziez,
> Si fu al flum d'enfern plungiez:
> Dur sunt li nerf, dures les veines,
> Que de vif sanc sunt tutes pleines. (86-90)

The use of superlatives to convey at times supreme richness and at times universality has already received comment, but it is

worth noting that Marie is alert to the variety of linguistic forms
that constitute this stylistic feature. Very often she uses the first
person to present this idea, usually negated, e.g.:

>Les altres drap ne sai preisier (*Guigemar*, 177)

>Un aigle d'or ot desus mis;
>Del cel ne sai dire le pris. (*Lanval*, 87-88)

>Ne sai mie les dras preisier (*Yonec*, 389)

Elsewhere she uses a form of antonymy:

>Deus chandelabres de fin or—
>Le pire valeit un tresor (*Guigemar*, 183-84)

while the idea of universality is conveyed either through
enumeration, as again in *Guigemar*:

>En Lorreine në en Burguine
>Në en Angou në en Gascuine
>A cel tens ne pout hom truver
>Si bon chevalier ne sun per. (53-56)

or through negation:

>Il n'ot un sul ki l'esgardast
>De droite joie n'eschaufast (*Lanval*, 583-84)

In addition, the superlatives may be either of unrestricted
application, e.g.:

>Suz ciel n'at or ki vaille plus (*Guigemar*, 158)

or restricted:

>El rëaulme n'en out plus bel (*Guigemar*, 38)

>Guilliadun ot nun la pucele
>El rëaume nen ot plus bele (*Eliduc*, 17-18)

The use of the first person as one means of expressing a
superlative is one indication of Marie's personal involvement
with the story she is telling, which adds to the liveliness of her
writing. The author's intervention is seen more often in her
exclamations, either to express her satisfaction at the progress of
her characters, e.g. 'Ore est Lanval en dreite veie!' (*Lanval*, 134)
or her foreboding in anticipation of a tragic outcome, e.g.:

>Mes jo creim que poi [ne] li vaille,
>Kar n'ot en lui point de mesure. (*Les deus amanz*, 178-79)

and

> Allas! cum ierent malbailli
> Cil ki l'un veut si agaitier
> Pur eus traïr e enginner! (*Yonec*, 254-56)

and

> Deus! qu'il ne sout la traïsun
> Quë aparaillot le felun (*Yonec*, 295-96)

where she is completely caught up in her own story.

In these and various other ways the author of the *Lais* is seen to be unobtrusively but undeniably present. The stories which she has taken from various sources she has transformed in her own way and she has lent them the stamp of her individual style of narrative and composition. As a result we see before us a fully unified collection of poems which is at once firmly established in the literary tradition and heritage of twelfth-century France and yet which cannot fail to appeal to those readers of the twentieth century for whom the delicate analysis of human love, that most enigmatic of emotions, retains its age-old appeal.

BIBLIOGRAPHY

1. Adams, A. and T.D. Hemming, '*Chèvrefeuille* and the evolution of the Tristan legend', *Bulletin bibliographique de la Société internationale arthurienne*, 28 (1976), 204-13.

2. Bambeck, M., 'Das Werwolfmotif im *Bisclavret*', *Zeitschrift für romanische Philologie*, 89 (1973), 123-47.

3. Baum, R., *Recherches sur les oeuvres attribuées à Marie de France* (Heidelberg: Winter, 1968).

4. Biller, G., *Etude sur le style des premiers romans français en vers (1150-75)* (Göteborg: Elanders Boktryckeri Aktiebolag, 1916).

5. Briffault, R.S., *The Troubadours* (Bloomington: Indiana University Press, 1965).

6. Bromwich, R., 'A note on the Breton lays', *Medium Aevum*, 26 (1957), 36-38.

7. Bullock-Davies, C., 'The love-messenger in *Milun*', *Nottingham Medieval Studies*, 16 (1972), 20-27.

8. —— 'The form of the Breton lay', *Medium Aevum*, 42 (1973), 18-31.

9. Burgess, G.S., *Contribution à l'étude du vocabulaire pré-courtois* (Geneva: Droz, 1970).

10. Cagnon, M., '*Chievrefueil* and the Ogamic tradition', *Romania*, 91 (1970), 238-55.

11. Chaucer, *The Canterbury Tales*, trans. by N. Coghill (Harmondsworth: Penguin, 1951).

12. Colby, A.M., *The Portrait in Twelfth-Century French Literature: an example of the stylistic originality of Chrétien de Troyes* (Geneva: Droz, 1965).

13. Coppin, J., *Amour et mariage dans la littérature française du nord au moyen-âge* (Paris: Librairie d'Argences, 1961).

14. Cottrell, R.D., 'Le lai du Laüstic: from physicality to spirituality', *Philological Quarterly*, 47 (1967), 499-505.

15. Cropp, G.M., *Le Vocabulaire courtois des troubadours de l'époque classique* (Geneva: Droz, 1975).

16. De Caluwé, J., 'La conception de l'amour dans le lai d'Eliduc de Marie de France', *Le Moyen Age*, 77 (1971), 53-77.

17. —— 'L'élément chrétien dans les *Lais*' in *Mélanges de littérature du moyen âge au XXe siècle offerts à Jeanne Lods*, I (Paris: Coll. de L'Ecole Normale Supérieure de Jeunes Filles, 10, 1978), pp. 95-114.

18. Delbouille, M., '*El chief de cest commencement* (Marie de France, *Prologue de Guigemar*)' in *Etudes de civilisation médiévale (IXe-XIIe siècles): mélanges offerts à E.-R. Labande* (Poitiers: C.E.S.C.M., 1974), pp. 185-96.

19. Denomy, A.J., 'Courtly love and courtliness', *Speculum*, 28 (1953), 44-63.

20. *Eneas: a twelfth-century French Romance*, translated with an introduction and notes by J.A. Yunck (New York and London: Columbia University Press, 1974).

21. Faverty, F.E., 'The story of Joseph and Potiphar's wife in medieval literature', *Harvard Studies and Notes in Philology and Literature*, 13 (1931), 81-127.

22. Fitz, B.E., 'The storm episode and the weasel episode: sacrificial casuistry in Marie de France's *Eliduc*', *Modern Language Notes*, 89 (1974), 542-49.

23. *La Folie Tristan de Berne*, ed. by E. Hoepffner (Paris: Les Belles Lettres, 1934).

24. *La Folie Tristan d'Oxford*, ed. by E. Hoepffner (Paris: Les Belles Lettres, 1938).

25. Foster Damon, S., 'Marie de France: psychologist of courtly love', *PMLA*, 44 (1929), 968-96.

26. Foulon, C. 'L'éthique de Marie de France dans le lai de *Fresne*', in *Mélanges Jeanne Lods*, I, pp. 203-12.

27. Frey, J.A., 'Linguistic and psychological couplings in the *Lays* of Marie de France', *Studies in Philology*, 51 (1964), 3-18.

28. Geoffrey of Monmouth, *The History of the Kings of Britain*, trans. by L. Thorpe (Harmondsworth: Penguin, 1966).

29. Green, R.B., 'The fusion of magic and realism in two lays of Marie de France', *Neophilologus*, 59 (1975), 324-36.

30. Hatcher, A.G., 'Le lai du *Chievrefueil*', *Romania*, 71 (1950), 330-44.

31. Hoepffner, E., 'Marie de France et l'*Eneas*', *Studi Medievali* (NS), 5 (1932), 272-308.

32. —— *Les Lais de Marie de France* (Paris: Nizet, 1959).

33. Hunt, T., 'Glossing Marie de France', *Romanische Forschungen*, 86 (1974), 396-418.

34. Illingworth, R.N., 'Celtic tradition and the lai of Guigemar', *Medium Aevum*, 31 (1962), 176-87.

35. —— 'La chronologie des *Lais* de Marie de France', *Romania*, 87 (1966), 433-75.

36. Ménard, P., *Les Lais de Marie de France: contes d'amour et d'aventure du Moyen Age* (Paris: PUF, 1979).

37. Mickel, E.J., Jr, 'Guigemar's ebony boat', *Cultura Neolatina*, 37 (1978), 9-15.

38. Nagel, R., 'A propos de *Fresne* (vv. 261-272)', *Cahiers de Civilisation Médiévale*, 10 (1967), 455-56.

39. Paton, L.A., *Studies in the Fairy Mythology of Arthurian Romance*, 2nd enlarged edition by R.S. Loomis (New York: Burt Franklin, 1960).

40. Payen, J.-C., *Le Motif du repentir dans la littérature médiévale (des origines à 1230)* (Geneva: Droz, 1967).

41. Pelan, M., *L'Influence du Brut de Wace sur les romanciers français de son temps* (Paris: Droz, 1931).

42. Pickens, R.T., 'Thematic structure in Marie de France's *Guigemar*', *Romania*, 95 (1974), 328-41.

43. Ringger, K., *Die 'Lais': zur Struktur der dichterischen Einbildungskraft der Marie de France*, Beihefte zur Zeitschrift für romanische Philologie, 137 (Tübingen: Niemeyer, 1973).

44. Robathan, D.M., 'Ovid in the Middle Ages' in *Ovid*, ed. by J.W. Binns (London: Routledge and Kegan Paul, 1973), pp. 191-209.

45. Sienaert, E., *Les Lais de Marie de France: du conte merveilleux à la nouvelle psychologique* (Paris: Champion, 1978).

46. Spearing, A.C., *Criticism and Medieval Poetry* (London: Edward Arnold, 2nd edn, 1972).

47. Sturm, S., *The Lay of Guingamor* (North Carolina: University of North Carolina Press, 1968).

48. Thomas, *Le Roman de Tristan*, ed. by B. Wind (Geneva: Droz, 1960).

49. Tobin, P.M., *Les Lais anonymes des XIIe et XIIIe siècles: édition critique de quelques lais bretons* (Geneva: Droz, 1976).

50. Webster, K.G.T., *Guinevere: a study of her abductions* (Milton, Mass.: The Turtle Press, 1951).

51. Wind, B., 'L'idéologie courtoise dans les lais de Marie de France' in *Mélanges de linguistique romane et de philologie médiévale offerts à M. Maurice Delbouille, II (Philologie Médiévale)* (Gembloux: Duculot, 1964), pp. 741-48.

Further reading

For a comprehensive bibliography of works on Marie de France published before 1976 see G.S. Burgess, *Marie de France: an analytical bibliography*, Research bibliographies and checklists, 21 (London: Grant & Cutler, 1977). The following is a short selection of items published since 1975, which have not been referred to in the course of this book:

Braet, H., 'Notes sur Marie de France et Ovide' in *Mélanges de philologie et de littérature romanes offerts à Jeanne Wathelet-Willem* (Liège, 1978), pp. 529-44.
Jonin, P., 'Merveilleux celtique et symbolique universel dans *Guigemar* de Marie de France' in *Mélanges Wathelet-Willem*, pp. 239-55.
——, 'Les préambules des lais de Marie de France', in *Mélanges Jeanne Lods, I*, pp. 351-64.
Knapton, A., 'La poésie enluminée de Marie de France', *Romance Philology*, 30 (1976), 177-87.

McClelland, D., *Le Vocabulaire des Lais de Marie de France* (Ottawa: Editions de l'Université d'Ottawa, 1977).

Payen, J.-C., 'Structure et sens d'*Yonec*', *Le Moyen Age*, 82 (1976), 263-87.

Ribard, J., 'Le *Lai de Lanval*: essai d'interprétation polysémique' in *Mélanges Wathelet-Willem*, pp. 529-44.

Yoder, E.K., 'Chaucer and the "Breton" lay', *Chaucer Review*, 12 (1977), 74-77.